THE OLD CORPS

THE
OLD CORPS

A PORTRAIT OF THE
U.S. MARINE CORPS BETWEEN THE WARS

By Brigadier General Robert Hugh Williams
U.S. Marine Corps (Ret.)

NAVAL INSTITUTE PRESS
Annapolis, Maryland

Library of Congress Cataloging in Publication Data
Williams, Robert Hugh, 1907–
The old corps.
1. United States. Marine Corps—History—20th
century.   2. Williams, Robert Hugh, 1907–
3. Generals—United States—Biography.   4. United
States. Marine Corps—Biography.   I. Title.
VE23.W47   359.9'6'0924 [B]   80-81090
ISBN 0-87021-504-3   AACR2

Printed in the United States of America

CONTENTS

FOREWORD

This is not an autobiography in the generally accepted sense of the word, but rather a collection of reminiscences, many delightful, some hilarious, of a junior Marine officer who served with pride in the *Old Corps* in the period between the great wars. Those who emerged from this period became what we know as "the Old Breed." There are not too many left, and their ranks are thinning.

To my knowledge no officer has, until the present time, recorded the daily life of that cloistered world. True, the initiates did not take the vow of celibacy, but they certainly took those of poverty and obedience. We are allowed to infer that these were not too onerous.

If there had been a motto for the Old Corps it would not have been "Gung Ho." It would have been "Excel," and that is just what marines of that time strove to do.

Another characteristic of the Old Corps about which Williams writes was "Trust." Men trusted one another, and they trusted their officers for the simple reason that the officers knew their stuff, and knew their men. This was not then a technological jungle with a "career counselor" sitting in a cubicle down the hall.

Yes, there was "spit and polish." Far too much of it, in fact. But there were gradations, and a little of that stuff never hurt. I believe there was a good balance.

Bob Williams, now a retired brigadier general with a distinguished record, has unlocked many doors to the Old Corps. It is a pleasure to open them and catch a glimpse of that distant and fast-disappearing past.

Samuel B. Griffith II
B. Gen., USMC (Ret.)

PREFACE

I have tried to describe life as I experienced it in the small Marine Corps that came to an end with the expansion for the Second World War. Since I was commissioned a second lieutenant in 1929, the first ten years of my service coincided with what may be considered the last decade of the Old Corps.

I am grateful to Brigadier General Edward H. Simmons, USMC (Ret), Director of Marine Corps History and Museum, for his encouragement and advice as well as for the research assistance afforded by personnel of the Marine Corps Historical Center, particularly Gunnery Sergeant William K. Judge, Chief, Still Photographic Depository.

Some readers may be disappointed to find only limited references to expeditionary duty in Haiti and Nicaragua and to Marine Corps aviation during the years of which I have written. I suspect that all marines over forty years of age, active or retired, have their own Old Corps. This was mine.

THE OLD CORPS

I

OFFICERS AND MEN

The leisurely pace of military life before 1940 is difficult to imagine today. Indeed, to many officers now on the retired list, service life appears less attractive than in their day. I suppose that the present as perceived by the elderly always suffers in comparison with fond memories of the past. The Second World War, however, did mark the end of an era for the Marine Corps, and for the larger services as well.

The Corps was much smaller during the period between the two wars than it has ever been since, less than 20,000. This meant that after a few years service, a young officer would know personally or by reputation most of those senior to him. He could easily keep track of his fellow officers by reading the weekly *Army and Navy Register*, which printed change of station orders and the names of those promoted and due for promotion.

In those days, there were fewer than 1,100 marine officers on active duty, in contrast to more than 17,000 today. It is noteworthy that there are roughly the same number of commissioned officers on active duty today as the total number of officers and enlisted marines of the old Corps at the depth of the Great Depression in the 1930s.

A stylishness uniquely military, swank as it used to be called, seemed to fade with the disappearance of riding boots and spurs when the Army abandoned the horse at the advent of the Second World War. A briefcase or some other useful object has replaced the riding crop and swagger stick. No longer is it enough to wear insignia of rank and service; an officer must also display a name plate like a delegate at a convention.

It was in the smaller Corps of the interwar period that I served as a young officer. In the late 1920s, second lieutenants were commissioned annually from the graduating classes of the Naval Academy, of military colleges such as Virginia Military Institute, and of universities that offered the Army's ROTC program. There were also always a few former enlisted marines who qualified for a commission by passing the difficult examinations required. I was commissioned a second lieutenant in 1929, following graduation from Ohio State University as an ROTC cadet.

Each September all newly commissioned second lieutenants were ordered to the Basic School at Marine Barracks, Navy Yard, Philadelphia. There the "gold bar cadets,"* as they derisively styled themselves, passed an academic year devoted to military studies which ended with six weeks of range firing and field exercises at Mount Gretna, the Pennsylvania National Guard camp.

I was one of fifty-three students, among them Samuel B. Griffith II,** assembled at the Basic School in 1929. At first the Naval Academy graduates, who had received unrestricted commissions, rather fancied themselves because the rest of us had two-year probationary commissions which could be revoked for cause by the Secretary of the Navy. We were also forbidden to marry until we had passed comprehensive examinations in military subjects at the end of the probationary period and received our unrestricted commissions. The few students from the ranks were a little older, with the advantage of Marine Corps experience. We university men were inclined to be respectful of both. Although we knew more about field soldiering than the Naval Academy graduates, we were unfamiliar with the naval service, Navy and Marine Corps, and our uniforms were still to be cut.

Four afternoons each week after classes that autumn, Anthony J. Drexel Biddle,† distinguished citizen of Philadelphia, taught us individual combat. He had had a reserve commission in the Marine Corps since the First World War. All forms of personal combat interested him, especially boxing and knife fighting. By adapting a boxer's footwork and the cut and thrust and parry of a fencer to bayonet fighting, he had

---

*Newly commissioned Navy ensigns and Army second lieutenants were ordered to duty aboard ship and to a regiment. Only the Marine Corps required its new second lieutenants to undergo a fifth academic year. A single gold bar worn on each shoulder was the second lieutenant's insigne of rank.

**Brigadier General Samuel B. Griffith II, USMC (Ret), of Newport, R.I., who has had two distinguished careers. After an active and varied twenty-seven years (1929–1956) of service in war and peace (Distinguished Service Cross, Navy Cross, Chinese language student in Peking), he attended Oxford University where he received the degree of Doctor of Philosophy. His second career has been that of translator of Chinese military classics (*Mao Tse-tung: On Guerilla Warfare, Sun Tzu: The Art of War*) and historian (*The Battle for Guadalcanal, In Defense of the Public Liberty*).

†Not the Tony Biddle, soldier and diplomat, that may come to readers' minds, but his father, 1874–1948.

Lt. Colonel Anthony J. Drexel Biddle, USMCR, demonstrating knife-fighting techniques to recruits at Parris Island. Courtesy U.S. Marine Corps.

developed a technique far superior to that set forth in the official Army manual.

Tony would arrive at the parade ground in a taxi which waited for him, wearing a sweat shirt and trousers, to find us already formed at wide intervals, similarly attired and armed with rifle and bayonet. Immediately he would discuss and demonstrate some fine point of bayonet fighting which we would then pair off to master. Occasionally he would bring a friend whom he would honor, and perhaps terrify, with the bayonet salute that he had taught us.

Once he brought a Colonel Drexel, probably a cousin of his and, like himself, well into middle age. At the end of the hour, our instructor wiped the sweat from his eyes and sang out, "Now, gentlemen . . . stand by. . . ." We knew what was coming.

"Bayonet . . salute!" Fifty-three young men, rifles carried at a high port (their rifle butts at waist level), rushed at and surrounded the visitor, crossing their bayonets in a rasping crash of steel above his head and bowler hat.

"Look out. Don't damage his hat," shouted Second Lieutenant Joe Tavern behind him as he brought the flat of his bayonet sharply down on it, shoving the brim over Colonel Drexel's eyes.

When the stock market crashed that autumn of 1929, we did not see our instructor Tony for three days.

After the First World War, the Corps was authorized twice as many regular officers as there were before the war. Consequently, there were vacancies comprised of the complete lieutenants' list and the lower two-thirds of the captains' list. These vacancies were eventually filled in 1920 by giving permanent commissions to several hundred officers who had served in the war with temporary commissions. Because so many officers received permanent commissions about the same time, the "World War Hump" was thus created, which stagnated promotion until the mid-1930s. Captains were often men in their forties with graying hair, expecting to retire as majors after thirty years service.

One could remain a second lieutenant for five or six years. The base pay was $125 a month. A complete outfit of leather and uniforms from the best military tailoring houses could cost $1,000. As the uniform was not worn after duty hours, however, except for official social occasions, officers also needed a civilian wardrobe including a dinner jacket. Only death or retirement for age or physical disability moved the sluggish promotion list, but there was interesting duty across the Pacific and bush warfare in the Caribbean where marine officers were detailed to serve as regular officers in the Garde d' Haiti and the Guardia Nacional of Nicaragua for a full foreign duty tour or even longer with increased rank and pay as incentives.

In 1931, a second lieutenant of two years service that had been largely academic, I reported for my first real duty at Marine Barracks, Norfolk Navy Yard, Portsmouth, Virginia. I had spent most of the academic year after Basic School at the Naval Air Station, Pensacola, Florida, where I failed my stunt check at Corry Field. The stunts I could do, but I had a tendency to "graveyard glide" (attempting to stretch a glide with a consequent loss of air speed and danger of stalling and crashing) when the check pilot cut the throttle to test my emergency landing responses with an idling engine. This convinced the board of naval aviators who sat in judgement on such matters that wings were not for me.

Without a doubt the board was correct. As the Basic School year ended, an increase in naval aviators was authorized for the Corps. All students who requested flight training and who passed the physical examination were accepted. Several of my classmates enthusiastically asked for it and became career naval aviators. Others, like myself, who saw it merely as an opportunity not to be missed, perhaps lacked the motivation and love of flying that characterizes all good pilots.

Within forty-eight hours of reporting to a new duty station, one had to change into white or blue uniform, depending on the season, to call and leave cards at the quarters of the commanding officer, and in this case, also those of the admiral, who was commandant of the naval district, and the captain of the yard. The bachelor officers, all second lieutenants, occupied a spacious house on officers row. Originally meant to be quarters for a field officer, the house today would be considered adequate for a three-star general. There had been no bachelor officers mess but we soon organized one. No enlisted cooks or stewards were authorized, so we hired civilian servants. There was a black cook at $1.25 a day who also did some cleaning and a laundress who ironed beautifully and waited on table.

Daily at 0800 we turned out for morning colors in stiffly starched khaki, brass and leather gleaming. We wore Sam Browne belts and breeches with high cut shoes and leather puttees, although field and general officers might wear riding boots and spurs. There were usually more lieutenants on the post than were needed to be in formation with the barracks detachment. Most of us stood morning colors as spectators, listening critically at the salute to the spirited call by the field music of the guard. The Barracks and sea school detachments were formed on the parade ground at present arms. After the flag was raised, the two detachments stood Troop and Inspection, that is, their rifles were inspected. This was usually followed by close order drill. This drill, based on an eight-man squad formed in two ranks, is said to have been introduced by the Baron von Steuben, George Washington's inspector general, during the Revolutionary War.

"Squads Ri-i-ght . . . March!" This command, given to put a unit in motion when halted in line with rifles at order arms, triggered a series of coordinated actions that now require three separate commands.

As immobility in line became a marching column moving off to the right, the rifles leapt from the ground with the first step to find their way miraculously to the right shoulder on the third. Simultaneously, each of the four squads of a platoon changed direction ninety degrees to the right in six counts, to step out on the seventh in column of squads. None of the eight members of a squad moved alike or took the same number of steps.

At the command of execution, number one of the front rank (the corporal squad leader) became a fixed pivot, facing right and marking time, while numbers two, three, and four angled right to reform abreast of him as before but in the new direction. Rear rank men trailed behind their file leaders. Each man had to mark time for one or more of the first six counts except the number four man of the rear rank who had to leg it to come up on the new line and continue the march in the new direction as the others stepped out on the seventh count.

Similarly the reverse. The platoon being in column of squads in march, to form line to the left and halt, the drillmaster would sing out,

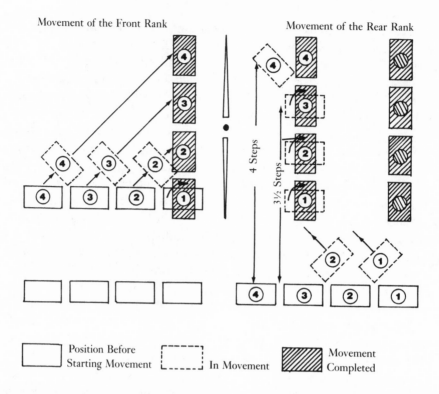

Movement of the Front Rank

Movement of the Rear Rank

4 Steps

3½ Steps

Position Before Starting Movement

In Movement

Movement Completed

Squads right (left) movement. The passage and diagram above, excerpted from the 1925 *Training Regulations* manual, "Infantry" section, describe how a squad, drilling alone or as any of the four squads of a platoon, either from a halt or in march, changed direction ninety degrees to the right on a fixed pivot. This movement was the essence of the old close-order drill which was abandoned for the simpler drill that has been in use since the late 1930s.

"Squads Left . . . March . . . Platoon (the preparatory command to halt, signalling the squads to continue to mark time at the count of six instead of stepping out on the seventh) . . . Halt! . . . one, two, one, two, three." Halting in line on the first two counts, the platoon would execute order arms with the following three counts.

So rich a repertory of drill movements did the drill manual provide that a spectator needed a technical understanding comparable to that of a balletomane to fully appreciate what he saw. In those days of simpler weaponry more time was devoted to drill. Perfection of execution was striven for and sometimes almost achieved during sweaty moments of rhythmic concentration when those in the ranks sensed the high quality of their performance under an exacting drillmaster. Right by Squads, On Right into Line, Squads Left About, Squads Right Column Right, Right

Front into Line—these were the commands, unheard now for more than forty years, that once rang out across old parade grounds.

Depending on how many lieutenants were available, one could have "the duty" (as officer of the day) every other day or as infrequently as one day in ten. Many young officers, including myself, did not own an automobile, sometimes because we were still paying for an initial full set of uniforms and leather. Thus, a quaint spectacle could often be seen: a second lieutenant wearing his sword, the ceremonial vestige that distinguished the officer of the day, while pedaling a bicycle about the yard to inspect sentinels on post.

Each morning at 1115 under the watchful eye of Captain Bower, the post adjutant, the old and new officers of the day marched abreast under arms into the office of the commanding officer, Colonel Robert Yancey Rhea, one to be relieved after making his report, the other to assume the duty. This was called the commanding officer's "office hours." If the commanding officer had something he wished to communicate to all officers, the bugler of the guard would sound Officers' Call beforehand. Each of us then proceeded to post headquarters to wait near the door of the colonel's office until Captain Bower invited us to enter and be seated in chairs placed against three of the walls.

After being relieved of the duty, one had the rest of the day free. Now and then one could request another afternoon off, but it was not a five-day week as now. Saturday morning was reserved for commanding officer's inspection, and Friday afternoon was field day (a curious nautical term) to prepare for it. On some Saturday mornings the Navy Yard Band would appear to play for a review and inspection, with the barracks and sea school detachments forming a rather understrength battalion.

After pay day, a monthly occurrence joyously heralded by sounding pay call, I proceeded to the naval hospital, located outside the yard, to pay the marine patients who were carried on our muster roll. Before doing so I had to put on a pistol belt with a .45 Colt Automatic with loaded clip in the holster.

For two or three months, I was a welcome visitor at the bedside of a marine named Hutchinson, one of two survivors of a patrol ambushed in Nicaragua. His right arm, having been almost blown off, was slow to heal. After the initial burst of hostile fire when the patrol entered the killing zone, the bandits showered the surprised marines with grenades. Hutchinson picked them up as fast as he could and threw them back until one burst as it left his hand. He was awarded the Navy Cross.

Commanding officer's office hours were also the occasion for dealing with offenders against good order and discipline. The colonel regarded five days confinement on bread and water (but with a full ration of three meals in the mess hall on the third day) as a salutary corrective for minor infractions. This punishment he could award without convening a court-martial. Most offenses were against good order without the gates, rather than against discipline within. This was a consequence of the men's condition: that of being single men in barracks who once a month had enough money in their pockets for a good overnight liberty.

The pay of a private was twenty-one dollars a month, that of a private first class, the highest rank usually attained during an initial four-year enlistment, was thirty dollars. The Marine Corps discouraged the marriage of enlisted men up to and including the rank of sergeant by simply ignoring its existence. A marine might marry but the Marine Corps would authorize neither family allowance nor transportation for his dependents when the marine was transferred. This was regarded as a sound restriction that saved the taxpayer a great deal of money by preventing young men from marrying before they could afford it.

From the time he completed his recruit training at Parris Island until the end of his enlistment, a marine was completely equipped as a rifleman, except for ammunition, to take the field on expeditionary duty. At boot camp he was issued a rifle, together with other articles of equipment such as a poncho, shelter half, bucket, canteen, and mess kit. The issue was recorded in his Service Record Book. Thenceforth he was held responsible for these articles until he turned them in at the end of his enlistment contract.

After initial issue, if a marine lost an article of equipment, or if he had to draw replacement items of clothing in excess of the annual allowance of about forty dollars, the cost was deducted from his pay. When transferred, an enlisted marine carried all his clothing and equipment on his back or in his padlocked seabag. Unlike his commissioned officers, who customarily changed into civilian clothes after duty hours except on board ship, he was forbidden to have any such clothing in his possession.

Venereal disease presented a serious problem to the military before penicillin came into use. Officially it was considered preventable through continence, or by the use of condoms sold at low cost in post exchanges, or by prophylaxis after exposure. For revelers returning from liberty late at night, the latter treatment, readily available at the sick bay, was duly recorded by the hospital corpsman on duty.

Venereal disease was difficult to conceal, because at irregular intervals a Navy medical officer would hold a surprise "short arm inspection" to discover sufferers who were trying to conceal their affliction. If there was no record of treatment, Navy General Order Number 20 required that an enlisted man forfeit a day's pay for every day of duty beyond one that he lost as a result of being on the sick list because of venereal disease due to his own misconduct. It was darkly suspected by many enlisted men of all the Services that saltpetre, believed to dull sexual desire, was mixed into their food.

In the minds of sailors and marines, apparently, the chief occupation of a Navy hospital corpsman was to treat and prevent venereal disease because they referred to him, jokingly and without malice, as a "chancre mechanic." While attending a staff college in England after the Second World War, I recalled this one day during an informal discussion, when someone mentioned British Army medics. I asked whether British soldiers had a nickname for them. "Yes," was the mirthful reply, "they call them prick farriers." Later, thinking it over, I concluded that the rank and file everywhere, past and present, must react similarly to the conditions and constraints of their occupation. Their characterizations, although fashioned in different tongues and times, were similar—earthy, tart, apt.

The Services were apolitical then. Few officers or men voted. For a marine to write a letter of complaint to a congressman was considered subversive, beneath contempt. Only whites were accepted for enlistment, so there could be no racial problem. An enlisted marine's relationship to his detachment or company commander suggested that of a subject to royalty. Other than saying "Good morning, sir," with his salute at the first contact of the day, he was to speak only when spoken to, and then should not introduce a subject of conversation, ask a question, or make a request.

To be sure, there were occasions when a marine appeared before his detachment commander to make a request, but this had to be arranged with the first sergeant. When a marine addressed an officer he used the third person. This required placing the article before his rank and omitting his name.

Once in Shanghai I overheard a first sergeant making sure that a young marine would observe the niceties of military courtesy for which the occasion called. "Now I'll be standing near the company commander's desk, and you're waiting outside the door, understand."

"Yes, sir."

"Don't say 'sir' to me. I'm not an officer. Say, 'Yes, first sergeant.' "

"Yes, first sergeant."

"All right. When it's your turn I'll say, 'Private Wilkins, march in.' What do you do?"

"I march in at attention and halt in front of the captain's desk."

"How far in front?"

"One pace."

"And with a good heel click."

"Yes, first sergeant."

9

"All right. When the company commander is ready to hear your request, what are you going to say? Say it to me now, like I was him."

"Sir, Private Wilkins has the first sergeant's permission to speak to the captain."

"Okay. Well . . captain is okay, but it's better to say company commander. He'll say, 'Yes, what is it?' Or maybe he'll just look at you and nod. Now what?"

"Sir, I request permission to change my allotment from . ."

"Okay, okay. He'll probably say, 'Permission granted.' Then what do you do?"

"I say, thank you, sir."

"All right, but don't mumble in there. Speak up! He might ask you a question or two. Just answer as best you can. When he is through, I'll say, 'About face. March out.' Let's see you do it now . . . ."

The term "officer and gentleman," now a quaint anachronism, was still in common use. In fact, there was a general charge in naval law, "Conduct unbecoming an officer and a gentleman." In one respect, however, an officer was treated by the rank and file more like a lady than a gentleman. Certain language was considered improper for him to hear. The lower ranks generally kept silent in the presence of commissioned authority, but if a sergeant felt a compelling need to use strong language, e.g. to express righteous indignation at a lapse on the drill field or a want of energy in a working party, he might with propriety resort to mild profanity in the hearing of an officer, but never obscenity.

There were fewer enlisted grades in the 1930s than now. The following table reflects the basic rank designations and pay scale of enlisted marines during the years between the two world wars:

	Per month
1st Grade: Sergeant major; quartermaster sergeant	$126
2d Grade: First sergeant; gunnery sergeant	$ 84
3d Grade: Platoon sergeant; staff sergeant	$ 72
4th Grade: Sergeant	$ 54
5th Grade: Corporal	$ 42
6th Grade: Private first class	$ 30
7th Grade: Private; drummer; trumpeter	$ 21

Staff non-commissioned officers (those of the top three pay grades) possessed, as they doubtless do now, a status in relation to the more numerous sergeants and corporals comparable to that of field officers to company officers. Exempt from guard duty, they were not required to fall in at mess formations and sat behind a screen at a special table at the far end of the mess hall away from the galley. There they could eat "early chow" if they wished. A marine could be well into his third four-year enlistment before attaining the third pay grade rank of staff or platoon sergeant.

Enlisted rank designations were generally the same as those of the Army except for the unique rank of gunnery sergeant. Until after the First World War, it was the rank of the third pay grade, below that of sergeant major and first sergeant. Functionally, gunnery sergeants were then platoon sergeants. Platoon leaders were normally second lieutenants, but sometimes one platoon of a company would not have an officer assigned and would be led by its gunnery sergeant. This had a curious effect. Perhaps feeling deprived at having no officer and realizing that their "gunny" was competing with officers, the members of such a platoon seemed to try harder to perform well.

A marine first sergeant was just what that rank designation implies. As in the Army, he was the senior non-commissioned officer at company level, but was primarily responsible for administration. As the burden of paperwork increased, the first sergeant was more and more confined to his desk. The need arose for another NCO to be moved up to the same pay grade as the first sergeant in order to project senior NCO authority to the drill field, the classroom, and the rifle range. In 1920 gunnery sergeants were moved up one pay grade to rank with first sergeants. Later another rank, staff or platoon sergeant, was created to replace the gunnery sergeant in the third pay grade.

A gunnery sergeant might be in his early thirties, fit, bronzed from the sun, taciturn rather than loquacious, possibly foreign born. He might roll his own cigarettes or smoke "tailor mades" (packaged cigarettes), or he might use snuff. This latter was not the powdered tobacco applied to the nostrils (a way of taking tobacco by that time long forgotten in America) but a substance more like chewing tobacco, a small cut of which was placed under the tongue.

Within the closed, stratified society of a company or detachment, both first sergeant and gunnery sergeant were obeyed with alacrity and accorded unfailing respect, but there seemed to be a more discernable warmth in the attitude of the men toward the latter than toward the first sergeant. Except on formal occasions he was addressed with friendly respect as "Gunny" by all ranks from commissioned officers to the youngest marines recently joined from boot camp. Whether wearing his field hat with khaki shirt and trousers or turned out in the martial splendor of undress blues, perhaps wearing the fourragère of the Croix de Guerre, he was the archetypal marine who confidently demanded respect from superior and subordinate alike, and received it ungrudgingly.

There were rare occasions of unit censure by a gunnery or first sergeant, or that even more impressive figure of the first pay grade, the sergeant major, with no officers present. Reciting a list of derelictions with heavy sarcasm, he would warm to his subject with a withering comparison of those facing him in ranks—inferior material which the commanding officer expected him to turn into an efficient detachment— with the capable, disciplined men of the *Old* Marine Corps. The recipients of this scorn would listen in silence, without recourse, as he bitterly explained how far their performance of duty fell short of his rightful expectations. If they had even been accepted for enlistment in the *Old* Marine Corps, which was unlikely, he might taunt them in conclusion, they would never have made it through boot camp.

In the 1930s, both officers and men often made reference to that Corps of the past, usually in jest and always stressing the adjective. Of course, to a young officer like myself or a nineteen-year-old private, the *Old* Marine Corps was simply part of an unremembered past which had no bearing on our lives. It was the Corps in which senior officers and NCOs had served before we were born, or the Corps which had sent a brigade to fight in France when we were children. We knew only the Corps of the 1930s in which we were serving.

I used to speculate about the image in the mind's eye of those admirable NCOs, on whose sleeves so many enlistment stripes were sewn, when they infrequently uttered those words seriously. Eventually I understood. Each generation of marines, as it reaches middle age after twenty years of service, acquires its own Old Corps, that of its youth. Its idealization is probably strongest if the earliest years of service preceded a wartime expansion.

Those senior NCOs of the 1930s were not recalling the Corps that provided half the infantry of the famous Second Division of the American Expeditionary Force in 1918. What they referred to was an apotheosis of the peacetime Corps in which they had served *before* the wartime expansion of 1917. The discipline and standards of the close-knit peacetime few cannot be transmitted in all their essence to the wartime many. With the return of peace comes contraction to another Corps of regulars. Regulars in name only at first, who in time will approach but never quite attain the remembered excellence of the Old Corps.

II

THE RIFLE

The Marine Corps made a cult of the rifle. Each year all officers and men under forty were required to fire the prescribed record course on the rifle range. No matter what else he might be, every marine was first a rifleman. Even aviation personnel had to fire the range annually; a marine artilleryman was as familiar with his rifle as with the howitzer he served. To hear anyone refer to the bolt action, .30 calibre, Springfield Rifle, Model 1903, as a gun, brought pitying frowns to the face of authority. It was a *rifle* and could only properly be referred to otherwise as a *piece*.

The secret of good shooting was simply stated, "hold 'em and squeeze 'em." If, while holding his breath, the shooter could gradually increase pressure on the trigger while he held the black dot of the bull's eye on top of the blackened front sight and lined up in the round aperture of the rear sight—and if he could hold steady without increasing or relaxing the pressure when the fidgety dot fell off, until he could persuade it back on its perch and resume the pressure—he would achieve a "surprise shot." Surprise, because by holding and squeezing instead of deliberately pulling the trigger, the shooter did not know precisely when the rifle would fire. Pulling the trigger deliberately when the sights were lined up on the bull's eye, a great temptation, invariably induced flinching in anticipation of the kick of the rifle butt on the shoulder when it was fired. The result of a surprise shot: a bullet hole in the center of the bull's eye, provided the rifle had been accurately zeroed and the wind correctly gauged.

For a month each summer post routine was disrupted when a fourth of the command was rotated each week to Fort Eustis, an Army post, to fire the range. This was preceded by several days instruction on the post parade ground. Turned out in campaign hats and padded shooting jack-

13

ets, marines practiced sling adjustment, getting into the proper firing positions, and sighting and aiming exercises.

At Fort Eustis those scheduled to fire the range were divided into two groups. Initially, one became the firing detail which was issued ammunition and proceeded to the 200-yard line. The other group became the butt detail which would raise and lower the targets and paste little squares of black or buff paper over the bullet holes after marking their locations for the shooters with the appropriate color-coded disk denoting a bull's eye (a solid white disk), a shot within the four or the three ring, or a lowly deuce. After this detail had disappeared into the butts, the firing detail was further divided into relays comprising as many shooters as there were targets.

Each shooter was then assigned a numbered target, and the first relay and the coaches took their places on the firing line. Slings were adjusted; as soon as the "A" targets with the smaller bull's eye were run up, firing could begin. No one in the butts could know to which targets his friends were assigned. Communication between the firing line and the butts was by field telephone manned by a disinterested member of the permanent range detail, who was also watched to assure that no shooters were identified over the wire. The second and third relays awaited their turn well behind the raised firing line, their rifle cut-offs raised and bolts locked open behind the magazine followers. These were safety measures to make doubly certain that no rifle could be fired accidentally behind the firing line.

Record practice consisted of 70 rounds in strings of 10 at four ranges. The total possible score was 350, a feat never accomplished so far as I know. Firing began at the 200-yard line with 10 rounds of slow fire from the offhand position (standing, using the hasty sling), followed by a string of rapid fire, with the shooter standing until the targets appeared, then shifting to the prone position, in one minute. "Ready on the left?" the officer in charge of the firing line would query through his megaphone. "Ready on the right?" Then, none having signified unreadiness, he would sing out, slowly and distinctly, the irrevocable words, "all ready on the firing line." This last, instantly repeated by the operator into his field telephone, signalled the officer in charge of the butts to blow his whistle to indicate that all targets, perhaps twenty, were to be run up, inviting a fusillade of 200 rounds during the next sixty seconds.

Next, it was back to 300 yards for ten rounds of slow fire, five at the kneeling position (the most awkward of shooting positions) and five sitting, followed by another string of rapid fire, with the shooter quickly changing from a standing to a sitting position when the targets appeared.

Slow fire, sitting and kneeling at 300 yards on the Quantico range about fifty years ago.

At 300 yards, the targets were lowered after a total firing time of one minute and ten seconds.

Then it was back to 500 yards for slow fire at the larger bull's eye of the "B" targets, with the shooter in the prone position, and the last string of rapid fire at the same but shrunken silhouettes, "prone to prone." That is, the shooter was permitted to get into the prone position, ready to fire, before the targets appeared. At 500 yards, the targets were lowered after one minute and twenty seconds. Finally, back to 600 yards, more than a third of a mile, for the last ten rounds of slow fire with a sand bag rest which made it easier for the shooter to keep his sights lined up on the bull's eye. More often than not this was a critical range for the shooter on record day. Knowing his total score up to that point, it was a matter of simple arithmetic to figure the minimum he must make at 600 yards to qualify as an expert rifleman or sharpshooter.

During rapid fire, instead of the round bull's eye of the "A" and "B" targets, there was a low silhouette representing the head and shoulders of an enemy rifleman in the prone position. The shooter tried to keep the front sight up in the black, squeezing steadily and rhythmically to distribute his shots evenly within the time allowed. After each round was fired he had to roll a little to the right in the prone position, keeping both elbows in place if he could, but certainly the left, to work the bolt. Withdrawing his trigger finger, he would release his right hand's easy grip on the small of the stock to seize the bolt handle. Jerking this up and back to eject the empty case, he would quickly shove it forward and down again to throw another cartridge into the chamber. Since a clip held only five rounds, he had to remove the empty one and replace it with another from his ammunition belt at about half time. Rapid fire called for intense concentration. For a minute or more a shooter was utterly oblivious to his surroundings except for the number of his target.

A miss at slow fire, considered shameful on the firing line, was marked with glee in the butts. Hearing the crack of a bullet and seeing no hole in their target overhead, the two marines serving, for instance, number seven would wait until the telephone operator called "mark seven." They would then pull the target down and scan it. Finding no hole, they would request verification by a lieutenant and then run the target up again. Across it, they would joyously wave back and forth a narrow red pennant affixed to a pole, a device known as "Maggie's drawers."

With a score of 306 or more, an enlisted man qualified as expert rifleman, earning a badge to be worn proudly and five dollars more pay a month. With a score of 290 or better he qualified as sharpshooter and three dollars more a month, but despite these incentives relatively few finished in the money. There was no extra pay for a third qualifying category—marksman at a 240 minimum—but overall, if training had been thorough, a command could qualify 95 percent of its personnel.

Headquarters Marine Corps analyzed closely the results of record firing. A post that qualified an unusual number of expert riflemen and sharpshooters, instead of eliciting praise, became the focus of dark suspicions that proper supervision had not been exercised to prevent "santa clausing"* in the butts. The Major General Commandant** might order an investigation which would include researching the scores made by

---

*A tendency of men in the butt detail to give shooters a higher mark for a bullet hole outside the bull's eye than was actually the case, e.g. to hold the four disk over a shot hole barely outside the four ring that was actually a three. Even one such assist could qualify a shooter for extra pay that he did not merit. The temptation was greater when marines working a target knew that a close friend was shooting.

**The rank of the officer serving as commandant, major general then, was included in the title in those days.

individuals in previous years. Whatever the findings, this would reflect on the commanding officer and the range officer.

It could be a long day on the range. Those who began firing at the 200-yard line ended the day in the butts. When the last target remaining up for the tenth round of slow fire at the 600-yard line had been marked, the butt detail busied itself with policing up as it awaited the final word from the firing line, "secure the butts," that marked the end of another day on the range.

During that summer of 1931 there was conjecture in the Bachelor Officers Mess concerning an officer due to report in to take command of the Barracks Detachment. When he arrived in September he appeared at first to be a modest man, a somewhat mistaken impression partially created by his poor English, which was so broken as to be barely understandable and sometimes mirth-provoking. Strangers did not particularly notice him until their gaze was drawn to his left breast, but he walked the earth apart. Captain Louis Cukela wore not only the ribbons representing two Congressional Medals of Honor, but also that of the *Legion d'Honneur*, awarded only to officers, and that of the *Medaille Militaire*, awarded only to enlisted men for acts of great bravery and to commanding generals of armies for great victories. A naturalized immigrant, Louis Cukela had enlisted in the U.S. Army in 1914. In 1916 while serving as a corporal in the Philippines, he learned that the Germans had captured his native village in Serbia and decided that he must fight them. Purchasing an early discharge, he returned to America with the intention of joining the Canadian Army, but the slogan "First to Fight" caught his eye. He enlisted in the Marine Corps in January 1917 and sailed for France in June, a corporal in the 66th Company, 5th Marines.

Cukela fought the Germans with hatred and ferocity, volunteering for dangerous patrols and raids in the hope of getting his hands on some of them, a fulfillment he reportedly realized several times. He was promoted to commissioned rank in the field after a daring exploit at Soissons for which he was recommended for the highest American and French decorations.

One winter day in Coblenz after the Armistice, Cukela, by then a lean, moustached lieutenant, stood smartly at the right of a line of persons to be decorated that included many field and general officers. General Pershing pinned the Medal of Honor, Army, above his left breast pocket and suspended the Medal of Honor, Navy, from the collar of his blouse.

Junior officers saluted Captain Cukela at a distance even beyond that within which salutes were ordinarily exchanged. One felt a little ridiculous while rendering the salute at eighty yards, but it would invariably be

Captain Louis Cukela wearing evening dress uniform about 1927. Courtesy U.S. Marine Corps.

smartly returned. In garrison he was a martinet whose displeasure it was well to avoid. Underneath, however, he was genuinely interested in the welfare of his men of whose peccadillos he was well aware. He was quick to anger, an anger that could flash to fury over what seemed trifles to others. Imperfections of dress and comportment, less-than-meticulous care of government property, or a breach of one of the many minor regulations, post orders, or customs that governed our lives exasperated him. To him they were enormities, thoughtless failures to measure up to the reasonable standards established by constituted authority. He looked upon an unbuttoned pocket flap, a perfunctory salute, or a speck of dust in a rifle bore as evidence that the individual concerned would be of doubtful value as a member of a reconnaissance patrol in hostile territory. Clearly, he felt, it was his duty to inculcate the young man with habits of neatness, obedience, and thoroughness so that in time he could be relied upon in a combat situation.

In 1931, Captain Cukela was past forty and no longer presented the physical appearance of a decade earlier. He would not again take the field on expeditionary duty, nor was he considered suitable for further military schooling. Despite his broken speech, however, his fourragère and his unique possession of the most distinguished French and American decorations, earned in a day when awards were fewer and made sparingly, commanded our awe and respect.

Another officer wore the fourragère at Marine Barracks, Norfolk Navy Yard. Captain Cukela and Captain Bower, the post adjutant, represented distinct types of career officers who, had there been no war, would never have been commissioned in the Marine Corps. George Bower, member of an old Philadelphia family, had graduated from Episcopal Academy in 1911 to continue his education at the University of Pennsylvania. He enlisted soon after the declaration of war and sailed for France as a machine gunner in the 5th Regiment. He was later commissioned a second lieutenant. At Belleau Wood a bullet wound in the left leg removed him from the fighting for a while, but he rejoined his company in time for Blanc Mont Ridge and the final war-winning drive of the Meuse-Argonne offensive. During the latter, he was nearly killed by a high explosive shell fragment that tore into his stomach only a few days before the Armistice.

He was the first officer I ever saw wearing a summer service uniform of gabardine. This light material required dry cleaning and was unsuitable for the field but, unlike khaki, it could be tailored to fit as closely as the wool cloth of the winter service uniform. All officers' uniforms were cut by a tailor then. This was before the demands of a larger service establishment following the Second World War would enable the ready-made clothiers to force such tailoring houses as Jacob Reed's Sons in Philadelphia and Brooks Brothers in New York to discontinue their military departments.

Captain Bower was a handsome figure in his gabardines, a swagger stick in his right hand or tucked under his left armpit, as he cheerily returned a salute on his way from his quarters on a sunny summer morning. He wore the ribbons of the Distinguished Service Cross, the Navy Cross, and the Croix de Guerre, won at some cost for he still suffered from the stomach wound and would soon leave the Service.

Post life was pleasant. Lieutenants reported in, sooner or later to depart for foreign duty, usually in Nicaragua. Our number varied from as few as three to more than a dozen in September. The country was well into the Depression, and for reasons of economy, the tours of officers on foreign duty were extended and those due for such duty received no orders for several weeks. In October there was an interlude off post.

Don Weller* and I were named platoon leaders of a provisional
company organized from the barracks detachment for duty during the
150th anniversary celebration of the surrender of Cornwallis. We camped
two miles below Yorktown, near the river, for three weeks to guard the
fuel depot and supplement the Marine Detachment, Naval Mine Depot,
Yorktown, in directing traffic and being polite to visitors. On the
anniversary of the surrender there was quite a martial display and President Hoover made an address.

Only 200 yards from our tents there was a pool where we cast for bass
in the early morning before breakfast. One evening we were invited to an
oyster roast out on a spit of land. Country people living near the mine
depot believed the locality was haunted by the military of long ago.
Strangely, it was not the redcoats or Washington's continentals that they
claimed to sometimes hear at night, but the hoofbeats of McClellan's
cavalry and the rattle of their sabre chains.

Earlier, back at the post, when the bachelor officers mess numbered
nine or ten, we gave a dance with a black band playing at one end of the
verandah. On another evening Colonel Rhea and Captain Bower dined
informally with us in civilian clothes. This came off well until shortly
after the meal when we began to hear faint intermittent sounds like the
popping of corks coming from the basement. The commanding officer
doubtless suspected that bottles of bootleg whiskey found their way into
the BOQ now and then, especially on weekends, but he never made any
effort to confirm his suspicions. At the same time, we were careful not to
confront him with lawless behaviour.

During the afternoon, on the advice of the officer of the day, whose
task it was to check the fermentation process, our bottling crew had put a
batch of home brew into several dozen quart bottles. In response to a
signal from the worried waitress from the pantry door, a second lieutenant
slipped down to the basement as the rest of us prepared two tables for
bridge. Contract had but recently replaced Auction in provincial bridge
circles.

When the troubleshooter returned, he grimaced ominously as he met
our questioning gaze. An embarrassing situation was in the making. I was
certain that I smelled beer after another flurry of popping noises. Colonel
Rhea's eyes met those of his adjutant.

"Well, gentlemen," said the commanding officer, "we must be off.
Thank you for the excellent food, but Captain Bower and I won't stay to

---

*Major General Donald McP. Weller, USMC (Ret), artilleryman, naval gunfire expert,
and horseman who won the Field Artillery Cup in 1936 while attending the Field Artillery
School at Fort Sill, Oklahoma.

play bridge tonight." To our great relief, both abruptly departed, probably vastly amused.

We rushed down to the brewery to be met with a disaster of flying corks and a floor drenched with sour-smelling foam that required some time to clean up. Our mess servants thought the whole episode to be hilarious, shrieking with laughter after noting that none of us took offense at their tentative giggles.

In November a major reported for duty as executive officer, so we had to give up the big house. Headquarters Marine Corps had resumed issuing orders for foreign duty and so few bachelors remained. Weller and Bunker Hill* and I moved into one of the vacant married officers' apartments. It looked as though Weller might soon be losing his freedom, as he was becoming increasingly attentive to Frances Jordan, a younger sister of the wife of the post quartermaster, First Lieutenant Matthew C. Horner, who of course was called Jack. A few days before Thanksgiving, Colonel and Mrs. Rhea invited the lonely bachelors to share their holiday turkey. Bunker and I gladly accepted.

Rumor persisted about an expeditionary battalion to be formed from East Coast stations, but there seemed to be no reason for one. We thought little of it until Colonel Rhea broke the news at his office hours toward the middle of December. "Well," he said, enjoying the moment, "I know you have heard some talk of expeditionary duty. Headquarters is putting together a provisional battalion to embark in the battleships *Arkansas* and *Wyoming*—the Training Squadron—soon after the holidays. Most of the personnel come from Quantico, some from Parris Island. We furnish four lieutenants—Donahue, Williams, Hill, Weller—and fifty enlisted. Temporary duty, of course. You will all be back here in March.

"Pretty fancy expeditionary duty! Andy Drum will be the CO. Some people are afraid of him. I've known him for a long time. He just goes by the book and expects everyone under his command to do the same. You will get in some weapons firing and small unit training at Guantanamo, but first the ships will go to New Orleans and Galveston for the last week of carnival. I don't know that it is a factor, but the Assistant Secretary of the Navy is from New Orleans and his daughter, I hear, is to be Queen of Rex. Oh, yes—uniforms. You take everything—whites, blues, khaki, of course, and mess jackets. Also swords. The orders will authorize second lieutenants to take two trunks, locker, [two locker trunks] instead of only one as allowed by the regulations."

---

*Brigadier General Robert E. Hill, USMC (Ret) 1907–1972, Naval Academy Class of 1930, who was awarded the Navy Cross twice for heroism while leading his battalion in the Guadalcanal Campaign.

III

VACATION CRUISES

Headquarters Marine Corps had authorized the organization of the 1st Battalion, 1st Marines in October. There was a machine gun company, "D," but only two rifle companies, "A" and "B." "B" Battery, 10th Marines, an artillery regiment, replaced "C" Company. Understrength at 338, the battalion arrived from Quantico before breakfast on 11 January 1932. After the officers and men of our contingent were added to "B" and "D" Companies, the battalion proceeded to Hampton Roads to embark in the *Wyoming* and the *Arkansas* in time for the evening meal. The following day the Training Squadron sailed for Charleston.

All of us from the Navy Yard were in the *Wyoming*. The others became machine gunners but I was assigned to lead the first platoon of "B" Company. Although Ernie Fry,* the other platoon leader, had been acting company commander, I was his senior and thus assumed the duties of that awesome office. These I carried out in accordance with the first sergeant's suggestions until Captain Donald Spicer brought the Parris Island contingent on board. A dark future awaited our company commander. Within a decade Spicer would be serving on Guam when the Japanese seized the island. He would be held prisoner by them for nearly four years.

The ships lay at anchor off Fort Sumter. Every day after breakfast, with the weather mild and the grass green, the ships' boats ferried the battalion to Fort Moultrie, the Army post on Sullivan's Island, for drill

---

*Colonel Ernest W. Fry, USMC (Ret), Naval Academy Class of 1930.

and instruction. We returned aboard ship for the noon meal, following which we received instruction of a seagoing nature. By 1530 I was again waterborne. With only the sketchiest knowledge of rowing acquired at the Basic School, I was detailed to form and train a "B" Company pulling whaleboat crew to compete with the other companies and "B" Battery in a race to be held at Guantanamo Bay.

I devoted all my liberty hours to Charleston, enchanted by the serene old city and its Georgian ambiance. A stroll along the battery, a long look at a stone house rising from the sidewalk with walled garden and wrought iron gate, brought to mind images of an opulent past, of great families nourished by a rich commerce with Europe and attended by numerous slaves in their town houses and on their plantations. I recalled reading that a young red-haired lieutenant named William Tecumseh Sherman had served at Fort Moultrie and moved freely in that most aristocratic society of the Old South. A battalion parade in honor of the commanding officer of Fort Moultrie ended our stay at Charleston.

We were at sea again on 27 January, on south to the Gulf of Mexico where the ships parted company for Mardi Gras, the *Arkansas* proceeding to New Orleans and the *Wyoming* to Galveston. Our ship berthed at a wharf along the waterfront near the business section of the Texas city. A day or two later a new German light cruiser, the *Karlsruhe*, with curiously offset turrets and officers' staterooms cleverly designed to save space, stood in to berth ahead of us.

Few of us knew much about Texas. Our trite assumptions of what Texans were like may have applied to those in many parts of the state but not to the people of Galveston. As guests of the city for a week we enjoyed an atmosphere much more like that of Charleston than we had anticipated. Galveston was old, worldly. Its society was more structured and formal than we had thought probable in a part of the country that was, until comparatively recent times, a frontier. At the same time the city was wide open, a good liberty port. There were houses of prostitution with girls in evening gowns. Drinks were mixed at soft-drink counters in the hotels, not with bootleg liquor but with Cuban rum and Scotch whisky. These were the lighthearted days of high carnival, but everything was in good taste and orderly.

The German officers added an old-world touch with their heel clicks and bows from the waist. Their captain had been a U-boat commander during the First World War. He must have sunk many Allied ships because on dress occasions he wore the sparingly awarded *Pour le Mérite*. The *Karlsruhe* sailed before we did. She had no marines to render honors and needed none. As she backed into the stream and turned to pass the *Wyoming*, her crew, armed with rifles, were at quarters. German sailors

24

must have been drilled as routinely as German infantry. The sharpness of their present arms would have done credit to the Brigade of Guards.

After a rendezvous at sea with the *Arkansas*, we proceeded to Guantanamo Bay for a month's training ashore. Many of us for the first time in our lives drank a cocktail legally, one properly mixed in a bar with liquor from bottles with brands which were famous but not very familiar to us. We had still been in our boyhood when Prohibition began. Every afternoon at 1630 the "cocktail boats" left for the beach—not the base but Cuban territory where there were bars. Captains and commanders, who rode in the gig, slaked their thirst at the Red Barn, while lower ranking officers went to Caimanera in a motorboat.

At the end of the first week of going ashore daily for intensive training in small unit tactics, we enjoyed a sense of accomplishment. Everyone who rated liberty went ashore on Saturday afternoon, enlisted men to visit the base and its recreational facilities, and officers, unless they had friends on the base, to patronize their Cuban haunts. About supper time events took an astonishing turn. An operational priority radio message from Washington directed that all marines be transferred to the *Arkansas* to sail for the West Coast without delay. The shore patrol rounded up all officers and men and returned them to their ships.

We were up all night, for much of the battalion's gear was on the beach or in the deep stowage spaces of the *Wyoming*. Mess accounts had to be settled and living compartments and other spaces used by marines had to be left spotless. Before our arrival, the scouting force had departed to join the battle force in the Pacific. Toward noon on Sunday, everyone had been transferred, including the *Wyoming*'s small marine detachment. (Although this later proved to be a mistake, it was included because the message had read "all marines.") After the noon meal, we fell in at quarters on the crowded main deck. With a blast of her horn rolling across the empty bay, the *Arkansas* got underway.

We transited the Panama Canal on 2 March and were a bit crestfallen when a turbine broke down in Gatun Lake. With help, the old battlewagon made it to the Pacific side, but she had to go into drydock at Balboa. Although the urgency of our situation had evaporated, we were happy to have an unexpected ten days in the Canal Zone with liberty call sounded daily at 1300. Visitor cards enabled us to use the facilities of the Union Club in Panama City, and there was nightly entertainment at Mame Kelly's Ritz where cards of introduction were not needed.

Apparently the *Arkansas* was to have sailed for Hawaii where the battalion would have been transferred to the aircraft carrier *Lexington*. Aboard her, we would have been ferried across the Pacific at 30 knots to reinforce the 4th Marine Regiment at Shanghai. An emergency had been

The training squadron, the *Arkansas* and *Wyoming*, with the Floating Battalion embarked, Guantanamo Bay, March 1932. Courtesy Major General Weller, USMC, (Ret.)

The Floating Battalion off-loading gear for the beach at Guantanamo Bay in March 1932. Courtesy Weller.

The U.S.S. *Arkansas* (BB-33) in Gaillard Cut, transiting the Panama Canal. Courtesy U.S. Naval Historical Center.

declared there when the Japanese landed 50,000 troops near the city, but the breakdown in Gatun Lake caused a change of plan. On 11 March the *Arkansas* sailed for the Puget Sound Navy Yard at Bremerton, Washington, for a six-week overhaul.

No quarters were available in the *Arkansas* for "B" and "D" Companies, formerly of the *Wyoming*. Most officers and staff NCOs doubled up with ship's officers and petty officers but Bunker Hill, Fog Hayes,* and the recently married Don Weller, Naval Academy classmates, were packed into an airless little interior space with a low overhead and bulkheads that slanted at odd angles. It was really a linen locker, which its occupants dubbed the morgue.

I shared the stateroom of a junior grade lieutenant named Karpe, nicknamed "Fish." Of stocky build, he was one of those efficient officers completely at home and content in a seagoing environment. Outgoing, with a ready smile and a quip for the unusual, he was everyone's friend. The men in his division regarded him as the best officer in the Navy. He had an eager curiosity about all things nautical, particularly in the ship in which he happened to be serving, and had earned the reputation of knowing everything there was to know about the *Arkansas*.

Many years later in the fifties we chanced to meet in the bar of the American Club in London. We recognized each other instantly although

---

*Lieutenant General Charles H. Hayes, USMC (Ret), Naval Academy Class of 1930, who subsequently had a fine career as a naval aviator.

The *Arkansas* at the Puget Sound Navy Yard, Bremerton, Washington, in 1932 when the Floating Battalion was embarked. Courtesy Weller.

he wore four stripes on his sleeves and eagles were pinned to my shoulder straps. It was during the early period of the Cold War. He was our naval attaché in one of those Balkan countries that had no navy and was in London to attend a conference at U.S. Naval Headquarters at Grosvenor Square. A year or so later I read in a newspaper that he had mysteriously lost his life aboard the Arlberg-Orient Express, in which he was returning home after a three-year tour of duty, while it was speeding through a tunnel in Austria.

The marines of "B" and "D" Companies had to sleep in cots placed in the air castles on the main deck, their sea bags suspended from the

Second Lieutenants Robert E. "Bunker" Hill, left, and Donald M. Weller of the Floating Battalion on board the *Arkansas* in 1932. Courtesy Weller.

overhead. A fortnight of discomfort intensified by extremely foul weather ended at Bremerton on 26 March. Our commanding officer, Lieutenant Colonel Andrew B. Drum, arranged for the battalion to fire the range at Fort Lewis, the Army post near Tacoma. Meanwhile, bluejackets transferred ashore for discharge were not replaced and marines were assigned to man half the main battery (an unusual, possibly unique assignment), which finally resulted in adequate living space aboard ship for all.

We began to refer to ourselves as the lost battalion on Noah's Ark, but the northwest corner of the country was new and interesting. Some of us took the ferry to Seattle to see Walter Hampden play *Cyrano de Bergerac*. If

I had not been ordered to Fort Lewis I would have repeated the trip to see Otis Skinner and Maude Adams in the *Merchant of Venice*.

Her overhaul completed, the *Arkansas* sailed south on 30 April to join the United States Fleet, battle force and scouting force, concentrated in San Francisco Bay. It was well worth climbing to the top of Telegraph Hill to see those sixty ships manned by 41,000 officers and men riding at anchor together. After passing through the Golden Gate, we were at quarters for an hour, rendering honors to many flagships, before the ship anchored at the end of battleship row. Unlike today, the great bay with its miles of wharves, landlocked except for the Gate, teemed with activity.

When the fleet departed for San Pedro on 12 May the married officers were gloomily convinced that the Floating Battalion, as it came to be called, would remain indefinitely on board the *Arkansas*. In no circumstances could temporary duty orders be extended beyond six months. Orders detaching us from home stations and changing our status to that of permanent duty were expected daily. This would require the families of married officers and NCOs to vacate government quarters without the help of the head of the family.

While this did transpire for most, Lieutenant Colonel Drum and Second Lieutenants Hayes and Williams were ordered to stand detached from temporary duty and proceed immediately to home stations to resume regular duties. This was great news for me as the Floating Battalion was becoming a bore. The experience of being a member of a battalion embarked in a battleship was growing old. "Expeditionary duty" meant performing main battery drills, normally a task assigned to sailors. Although this interested my Naval Academy friends, my reaction could be compared to that of a mounted field artilleryman who had been assigned to the dull, fortress-bound Coast Artillery. "B" Company was only at half strength, forty men having been transferred to a replacement draft for China.

Individual travel orders to cross the continent were rare, especially for second lieutenants. The lucky recipient was expected to travel first class as befitted an officer and a gentleman. This he could do at eight cents a mile, even on a crack extra fare train, and be well in the black with about $100 to spare at the end of the journey. The pay officer at the point of origin provided the rail ticket and some advance pay, if needed. At the destination one received the balance of the sum due in cash. I boarded the famous Santa Fe Chief for Chicago on 30 May. From there, traveling via Columbus, Ohio, with a stop overnight to visit my parents, I arrived back at the Norfolk Navy Yard on 4 June 1932.

Although I was a welcome addition to the duty roster, no one could explain my sudden reappearance. It was not clear until a week later when typed orders arrived from the Major General Commandant. I was directed to embark in the U.S. Naval Transport *Henderson* on or about 7 July 1932 at the Naval Operating Base, Hampton Roads, Virginia, for transportation to Shanghai, China, for duty with the 4th Regiment. Here we go again! I had read in the Army & Navy Register that Fog Hayes had been ordered to the Nicaraguan Electoral Mission, which left me wondering as to the reason for my good fortune. I found out a day or two later when I received a brief personal letter from a senior officer on duty at Headquarters Marine Corps. The letter was the result of a small service I had performed for Colonel Rhea several months earlier. It was one of those little things that ultimately change the course of one's life.

One morning before I left with the Floating Battalion, Colonel Rhea had sent for me. When I presented myself at the adjutant's office, which was next to that of the commanding officer, Captain Bower said, "Have a chair, if only for a moment. I don't know what the colonel wishes to see you about, do you?"

"No, Sir," I replied a little uneasily, for it was unusual for the commanding officer to wish to see a second lieutenant.

"Well, stop in here again after you leave his office and let me know, unless of course it's a confidential matter."

"Aye, aye. Sir." To perform his duties properly an adjutant had to know the CO's intentions. Captain Bower quickly opened the connecting door, strode in to make known my presence, reappeared in the doorway to bid me enter, and retired to his own office.

"Ah, Williams," the colonel greeted me, "I wonder if you can help me out in a small matter. I've received a letter from a friend of mine at headquarters asking me to have one of my young officers meet a lady who returns from Europe tomorrow in the *City of Hamburg*, one of those small Baltimore Mail Line ships. You will just need to help her through customs and put her on a train to Washington. I don't know her personally, but she is traveling alone and will be expecting a marine officer to meet her. The ship will dock about ten o'clock. I'll tell the adjutant to provide you with transportation. You can't offer her a ride, of course. Go to the station with her in a taxi and have your transportation follow you. Her name is Mrs. Olmstead. There won't be many passengers disembarking. Just watch out for an unattended lady and present yourself as coming in my behalf. Any questions?"

"No, Sir."

Apparently I accomplished my mission satisfactorily. Colonel Rhea's friend at headquarters wrote notes of thanks to both of us, suggesting to me that I let him know when he could be helpful in the way of duty assignments. Earlier a new language-study opportunity involving two years residence in Spain had attracted me and I had officially requested it. Although I would never meet him, I wrote to him about the language detail and forgot about it when ordered away on temporary duty. This was the reply I received:

Dear Williams,

After receiving your letter several months ago I looked into the language detail you requested and found that, while you were eligible, it was thought better to assign an officer who had served in Nicaragua. In the meantime you were ordered to temporary duty afloat.

You should have more experience with troops before assignments such as you requested. The 4th Marines in Shanghai will provide this and I know you will enjoy serving in China.

So Fog Hayes and I went through the canal a second time in the same direction. There were other naval transports, but the one in which all naval personnel hoped to travel was the U.S.S. *Henderson*, affectionately called the Hendy Maru. On her maiden voyage, in June 1917, she sailed from New York with the 2nd Battalion, 5th Marines embarked, in the convoy that carried the first contingent of American troops to France. During the months of war she shuttled between New York and Saint Nazaire carrying marine battalions and replacements. After the war she abandoned her Atlantic crossings for the Pacific.

Year after year she leisurely steamed down the East Coast, through the Panama Canal, and up the West Coast to the Mare Island Navy Yard in San Francisco Bay, thence across the Pacific to the China Coast. It was a pleasure cruise on board the *Henderson*. Despite Prohibition and an earlier regulation forbidding possession of alcohol in ships of the Navy, it was understood that officer passengers might bring liquor on board. The presence of officers' wives and sometimes a grown daughter in a naval ship was a delightful anomaly. Senior noncommissioned officer and petty officer passengers were quartered below the main deck with the ship's petty officers. Some would have wives and children traveling with them, necessitating an awkward arrangement. Their dependents were assigned officer passenger state rooms on the main deck and took their meals at an early sitting in the wardroom. For two hours each afternoon at sea, the married NCOs were permitted on the main deck to visit their families.

We arrived at the Panama Canal too late in the day to begin transit, and so anchored off Cristobal. Several of us went ashore after supper. Unlike Panama City, Cristobal was not much of a liberty port but we wandered about, visited some bars, and returned aboard ship in a merry mood. Fog and I entered my stateroom, of which I was the sole occupant

The *Henderson* in 1933. Courtesy U.S. Marine Corps.

at the time, lifting our voices in song. The last thing I recall was Swede Larson* coming in and asking us to be quiet . . . .

When I awoke I sensed that the ship was docking. Looking upward to my left I saw Fog and wondered who he was. Remembering, I wondered why he had spent the night in my room. He was bare to the waist, lying on his left side in the lower bunk, facing the bulkhead. A grid of welts covered his back. I could not account for this disfiguration, nor could I understand why I had to look up, above eye level, to see a man in a lower bunk. Shifting my gaze to look straight ahead I saw the overhead. Fog turned over, peered down at me, blinked his eyes and burst out laughing. It occurred to me that I had gone to sleep while sitting in a chair, but something still puzzled me as Fog sat up and put his feet on the deck, still laughing. Then I realized that the chair in which I had slept, instead of

*Colonel Emery E. Larson, USMC, 1898–1945, Naval Academy Class of 1922, who captained the great football team of 1921 and returned to Annapolis in 1939 as a major to be head coach. At this time, before the adoption of the selection system of promotion, he was only a first lieutenant after ten years service.

33

having its four legs on the deck, was on its back. I was sitting in it all right, legs crossed, but the back of my head and my outstretched arms lay on the floor of the stateroom.

"All right, wise guy," I laughed in return. "Take a look at your back in the mirror." The welts were no longer a mystery. I preferred to sleep in upper bunks, so the lower had neither bed clothes nor mattress. Fog had slept on bare springs. Glancing at his wrist watch, he left for his own room. "See you on deck in half an hour?"

I nodded. It was mid-afternoon and the ship was docked in Balboa. We had missed transitting the canal. After shaving and showering it would be time to renew our aquaintance with Panama City, but first we had to fill in the blank of the night before. Casual inquiry gathered no intelligence until, a little diffidently, we approached Swede Larson whom nobody could dislike. He informed us with a smile that having failed to persuade us to be quiet the previous evening, he had put a hand behind each of our necks and bumped our heads together—gently at first, but then more firmly—and helped us sink to rest in chair and bunk. I must have tipped my chair over later, after he had left us to our slumbers.

The ship called briefly at Corinto, the port of Managua on the west coast of Nicaragua, to disembark personnel assigned to the Electoral Mission. I did not see Fog again for many years. Duty free liquor could be purchased near the pier. After discreet inquiries, ten or twelve passengers subscribed to a bulk purchase; as the junior officer I was detailed to consummate the deal. That afternoon a second lieutenant of marines might have been observed leading a file of stevedores toward the ship, each bent low under two cases of whisky slung over his shoulders in a length of burlap that concealed the labels.

Up the gangplank to the quarterdeck I marched, saluting and reporting my return to the officer of the deck, a middle-aged mustang,* who grinned broadly. I led the bearers to my stateroom where they stacked the contraband. After rewarding them and conducting them to the crew's gangplank I returned to receive callers.

Directly after the ship got underway a curious notice appeared on the passengers' bulletin board. It announced that passengers' staterooms would be inspected at 1000 on each of the following two mornings. Word was passed quietly that hand luggage and trunks were to be opened on the first day, but not bureau drawers. On the next day, the contents of drawers would be inspected but luggage need not be opened.

---

*Before the Second World War the line officers of the Navy were generally Naval Academy graduates. The few commissioned from the ranks, most of them during the First World War, were known as mustangs.

I was once again within the Golden Gate, with a week to explore the bay area while the *Henderson* was readied for crossing the Pacific. More officers and dependents reported on board. The lower deck compartments were soon filled with enlisted passengers, who would replace those completing their tours of foreign duty in the Orient whom the *Henderson* would bring home on her return voyage. Headquarters Marine Corps had decided to bring the 4th Regiment to peacetime strength by sending out the personnel to form a third battalion. We were a shipload of regular service people, Navy and Marine, officer and enlisted, wives and children. We would not see the United States for three years, but that was no cause for gloom. Most of us were bound for the China Station, a highly desired foreign service experience. We all looked forward to a leisurely crossing to congenial duty in distant seas and lands where one's dollars were said to go much farther than at home.

We reached Honolulu and then Guam, the latter governed by a U.S. Navy captain in those days. I recall enjoying cool drinks late in the evening with Lieutenant Colonel Benjamin S. Berry, who commanded the marine barracks. As a major he had commanded the 3d Battalion, 5th Marines, at Belleau Wood in 1918 where he was badly wounded. His battalion suffered heavy losses in the first gallant but unsuccessful attack across the wheat field.

The food was of a high order in the *Henderson*'s spacious wardroom which also served as the passengers mess. Because of her regular calls at so many ports across half the world her cooks and stewards knew where to obtain the best local vegetables and fruits. The morning after leaving Guam we breakfasted on succulent papaya. The cost of our food was $1.50 a day, payable in advance, but we did not really pay for it. Upon reaching one's destination and reporting for duty, one submitted a claim and was reimbursed. The pre-payment was a loan without interest required by the Navy Supply Corps. Although I never quite understood the reason for this financial arrangement, it probably provided the working capital to purchase produce and special foods at ports of call.

The monotonous days at sea were pleasantly idle. One read, talked shop, played bridge. A small unobstructed space on the boat deck was used for exercise. Enlisted passengers were brought up in groups during the day until 1600 when it was reserved for officers. We skipped rope, did calisthenics, and heaved the medicine ball.

Toward 1700 the more enthusiastic of us would rig a volley ball net. A regulation ball would soon have been lost over the side, so we used a medicine ball which could be heaved over the net only with the use of both arms. Although this variant of the game never became an Olympic event, it provided us with a great deal more exercise than if we had played with

35

the standard ball. At 1730 we descended to shower and dress. The second sitting of the evening meal began at 1830 (the wives of staff NCOs and all children were served earlier) so the preceding half hour or more was reserved for the tinkling of ice in tall glasses in the staterooms.

While the ship rode at anchor in Manila Bay for several days, many of us moved ashore to stay at the Army and Navy Club, that pleasant gathering place so far from home for American officers. One Sunday afternoon I was taken to watch a polo match. On another day I attended a Filipino wedding reception where I was presented to a slight, quiet man no longer young, General Aguinaldo, leader of the Insurrection in 1899. We then began the last leg of the long summer cruise. The *Henderson* headed north for the mouth of the Yangtze River. On 19 September 1932, she entered the Whangpoo River to discharge most of her passengers at Shanghai. We anchored in the stream at first, awaiting a pilot. It was early but a strange excitement caused me to rise and throw on a dressing gown to go on deck. I looked over the side to see a swarm of sampans manned by rivermen of an ancient race. I had reached the East.

IV

SHANGHAI

The first permanent Marine Corps station in China was in Peking, where the Legation Guard was established in 1905. This became the Embassy Guard in 1935. Unlike the small marine detachments in U.S. embassies today, the Embassy Guard was comparable to an infantry battalion, capable of defending the embassy compound for a limited period. Together with the troops attached to the embassies of several European countries and Japan, it provided some protection to the diplomatic community without dependence on Chinese assistance.

In 1927, when civil war in southern China menaced Shanghai, a provisional brigade organized from detachments in Guam, the Philippines, and ships of the Asiatic Squadron landed in Shanghai in January. The 4th Regiment from San Diego soon followed. Shortly thereafter, Washington decided to enlarge the force in China to a provisional brigade of all arms and Brigadier General Smedley D. Butler arrived in March with the 3d Brigade staff. In May, the 6th Regiment, together with artillery, engineers, and two aviation squadrons whose aircraft were disassembled and crated for the sea voyage, arrived to complete the brigade.

When the fighting moved north that autumn, the 3d Brigade went north to Tientsin to protect the line of communication to Peking, leaving the 4th Regiment in Shanghai. In 1928, the danger past, the brigade returned home, but the 4th Regiment stayed on as a permanent garrison in Shanghai.

In those days the Shanghai waterfront, or the Bund as it was called, was a scene of endless activity during the working day. Merchant ships, warships, sampans, junks, and motorboats filled the river. Rickshaws, taxicabs, soldiers, sailors, seamen of many nations, and Chinese hurried

37

Horse marines! The mounted detachment, Legation Guard, Peking, mounted on China ponies that stood about 12½ hands. At the upper left is the Ch'ien Men gate tower. Courtesy U.S. Marine Corps.

A marine of the mounted detachment, Embassy Guard, Peking, and his pony in the 1930s. Courtesy U.S. Marine Corps Museum.

A frequent sight in Shanghai during the 1930s. Marines marching along a street of the International Settlement. This appears to be the tail of a battalion column, with the last rifle platoon in the foreground and the machine-gun company (note the carts) bringing up the rear. Courtesy U.S. Marine Corps.

The Bund, Shanghai, about 1938 with the U.S.S. *Augusta* anchored in the Whangpoo river. Courtesy U.S. Naval Historical Center.

Map of Shanghai. Courtesy Library of Congress.

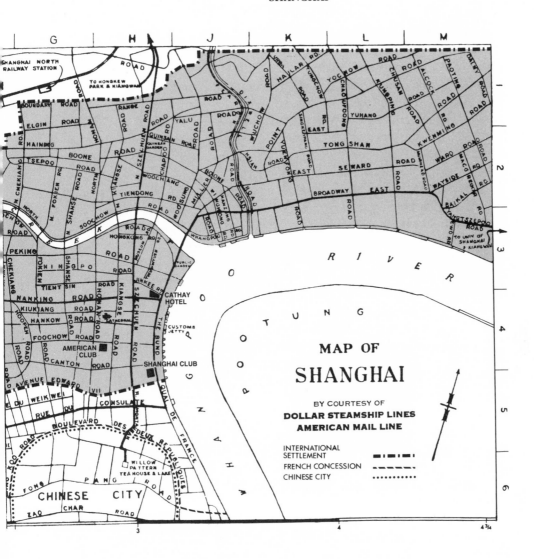

MAP OF

SHANGHAI

BY COURTESY OF

DOLLAR STEAMSHIP LINES
AMERICAN MAIL LINE

INTERNATIONAL
SETTLEMENT
FRENCH CONCESSION
CHINESE CITY

along the streets. Downtown Shanghai was noisy. Chinese pedestrians could never be persuaded to stay on the sidewalks, or that streets were for motor cars and rickshaws. Chinese taxi drivers honked their horns continuously while good-natured Sikh policemen* (who always said "hello John" to marines and were so greeted in return) controlled traffic with calm efficiency. Shanghai, a Western-style city built in China, was in the thirties one of the world's great centers of commerce. A splendid view of the waterfront activity could be enjoyed from a large window in the bar of the Shanghai Club near the Customs Jetty.

The essentially British and American International Settlement, along with the French and Japanese Concessions, comprised the commercial and foreign residential core of Shanghai. Extra-territorial rights were exercised on those few square miles of Chinese territory. Law enforcement was a function of the British-administered Shanghai police force. Americans and British had their own courts. Britain and the United States maintained consulates and several other countries had consular representation in the International Settlement within which all foreigners except the French and Japanese and also large numbers of Chinese lived. There were only about 10,000 British and Americans, whereas the population of Greater Shanghai was perhaps two million. There was a Chinese mayor, but he had no authority over the International Settlement, which was governed by a city council of British and American nationals.

There was also a White Russian community, most of whom were poor and unemployed except for those who served in the Russian Regiment, a mercenary unit of the Shanghai Volunteer Corps, or who played an instrument in the symphony orchestra. Many Russian girls worked nightly as paid dancing partners in the cabarets.

By western standards, Chinese labor was extremely cheap, making possible the attractive and inexpensive life that occidentals enjoyed on the China Coast. There were no white servants or artisans. At eight or ten cents an hour, an American blue-collar worker such as a carpenter could not have earned a living by U.S. standards, at least not at his trade. Most of the white-collar class were also Chinese. If you entered an American bank, the teller whom you approached would be a Chinese. Although he would be dressed in western clothes and would speak fairly good English, he would make calculations with an abacus.

Although the International Settlement was not a colony, the extra-territorial rights enjoyed by foreigners reduced the Chinese, even the

---

*Retired NCOs of the British Indian Army who were recruited for the Shanghai police force.

Marine cavalryman! A private first class, who appears to have the poise and bearing of a senior NCO, of the Mounted Detachment, Embassy Guard, Peking, in 1935. Courtesy U.S. Marine Corps.

rich, to an inferior status. Chinese were not admitted to any of the foreign clubs. A foreigner on the China Coast, like a China pony, was called a "griffin" for his first year. Initially, he might be mildly shocked at certain aspects of life as he found it there, for instance, by his first experience riding in a rickshaw pulled at a run by a barefoot youth in faded blue denim shirt and shorts who would probably not live to be thirty. Most

Typical Shanghai rickshaw boy hauling marine after a heavy rain, Shanghai, 1937. Courtesy U.S. Marine Corps.

foreigners, however, quickly adapted to their status as members of a privileged caste. None did manual work. Housework was done by Chinese servants who were paid much less for a month of thirty twelve-hour working days than a cleaning woman in the United States now receives for one seven-hour day.

Houseboys and waiters, required to wear white cotton gowns and gloves, were addressed as "boy," unless one knew their names. They spoke a quaint, obsolescent pidgin. Bobby Denig* and I shared a house-boy, Ah Fong, in the bachelor officer quarters at the officers' club on Seymour Road. I have never forgotten how this patient Chinese, perhaps forty-five and a grandfather, gently reproached me one day. Irritated with him for having forgotten some trifle, I reproved him while he was drawing a bath. This being more severe in his judgement than his lapse warranted, he calmly remarked, after turning off the water, "alla time trouble-trouble, alla time God damn." I apologized.

Most of my fellow passengers were assigned to the new 2nd Battalion but I was directed to report to the 3d, commanded by Lieutenant Colonel William C. Powers. I became a platoon leader in the 22nd Company,

*Brigadier General Robert L. Denig, Jr., USMC (Ret), Naval Academy Class of 1932.

An infantry company at peace strength consisting of two platoons of four eight-man squads. "L" Company, Captain John A. Tebbs commanding, was a few men under strength when this photograph was taken in the Jeanne d'Arc Compound in 1934. Courtesy *Leatherneck* magazine.

which soon changed its name to "L" when Headquarters Marine Corps adopted the alphabetical designations used by the Army. The battalion was billeted in two walled compounds facing each other across Moulmein Road.

In addition to a stone house, the General Lu Compound, formerly a residence, had two or three smaller structures, one of which served as battalion headquarters. My platoon was quartered in second-story rooms looking inward on an open court. The rooms were said to have housed the general's concubines. The Jeanne d'Arc Compound had been a Christian school for girls. Its dining hall and kitchen became the general mess, its playground the drill field.

Troops in formation had to remain within the boundaries of the settlement. It was therefore impossible to hold field exercises at regimental, battalion, or even company level. Jessfield Park, about the size of two city blocks and located near the western boundary of the settlement, could occasionally be used for platoon exercises. This constraint on normal field training fostered two characteristics of military life in Shanghai—spit and polish, and leisure. The international character of the foreign military presence contributed to the former (bayonets were nickel plated). Duty hours from 0800 to noon made possible the latter. Each company devoted one morning each week to a route march, swinging along the less-traveled streets at "route step, keep step." Every Thursday all three battalions marched to the race course for a regimental parade. On alternate Fridays the regiment executed Plan "A," its assignment for the defense of the International Settlement. Fully equipped for the field, the regiment

Shanghai street scene. The 3d Battalion, 4th Marines, returning to billets after Memorial Day services in 1933.

A Marine sergeant in winter service field uniform with overcoat on Soochow Creek when the 4th Marines manned their assigned defense sector to protect the International Settlement early in 1932. Courtesy U.S. Marine Corps.

manned the sector along Soochow Creek which it had occupied for several months during the fighting between Japanese and Chinese troops before my arrival. Those Friday mornings were smelly because of what was referred to euphemistically as the "night soil." Human waste, collected early each morning from thousands of Chinese families, was hauled in pushcarts (marines called them honey carts) to ordure stations along the creek. Here it was loaded onto barges for removal to fertilizer processing plants outside the city.

A patrol from the 4th Marines along Soochow Creek during the Sino-Japanese "Trouble" in 1932. This is how marines were uniformed for field service in winter before the day of the utility uniform. Courtesy L.H. Howard, USMC (Ret).

Before the day of the utility uniform. "L" Company at "route step, keep step" in a Shanghai street in the days of puttees, leggings, and Sam Browne belts. Note the ranks of four when marching in column of squads under the old "squads right" drill regulations.

A platoon of L Company passing in review at a regimental parade at the Race Course, Shanghai, in 1933. Part of the regimental band may be seen beyond the left flank of the platoon, facing the reviewing stand. The uniform is winter service green with barracks caps and leggings and officers armed with swords. Because enlisted men were not issued the blue uniform, this was the best the 4th Marines could do in the way of a dress parade. Note the care obviously taken in putting on the leggings to avoid any bagging of the trousers at the knee, or blousing over the tops of the leggings.

4th Marines' ammunition trailers pass in review. In the days before mechanization, Marine machine-gun companies hauled their weapons and ammunition in carts. Courtesy Clem D. Russell.

Drum, Bugle, and Fife Corps, 4th Marines, Shanghai, 1930. A battalion of the Green Howards Regiment of the British Army presented the 4th Marines with fifes and taught the trumpeters how to play them. Thus, the shrill and lively sound of those instruments, the only ones authorized by Congress in 1798 for the Marine Corps and since fallen into disuse, were heard again on the parade ground. Courtesy Clem D. Russell.

Afternoons were for recreation and athletics. American football was not played in Shanghai except for a nostalgic, pickup game played on Thanksgiving Day, so the 4th Marines fielded a rugby team which proved to be a great success year after year. Although the city was horsy, what one rode was not a horse but a China pony of 12 to 12½ hands. Not bred and trained, these ponies were captured and broken after six or seven years of running wild in Mongolia.

Twice a year there was a drawing by lot for ponies. One could subscribe for fifty dollars Mex (about ten dollars U.S.) a pony. The distribution of the better and the less desirable mounts was thus by chance. A "griffin" was first tried out for racing. If not fast enough, he might be suitable for polo, although it was all but impossible to train most of these ponies to turn quickly. They were given to turning in wide sweeping arcs at a gallop which no horsemanship could change to a collected stop and turn. If unfit for racing or polo, the new pony was used for paper chases or recreational riding.

Racing was on a grand scale, with gentlemen jockeys for the most part. The Shanghai Race Course was comparable to those in Europe and America. Three or four race meetings of four or five days were held each year. The Chinese loved to go to the races. Thousands attended, filling the public stands; between races they stood in long lines before the pari-mutuel windows.

Polo was played at another race course, Kiangwan, a few miles from Shanghai. There were several teams of business and professional men. Sometimes a British battalion would field a team. For two or three years the 4th Marines participated. The officers of the regiment subscribed to a fund to purchase ponies for the few who played. None of our officers ever played for Shanghai in the big matches with Hong Kong, Tientsin, or Peking, but one of our ponies, Auburn, would invariably play in every other chukker. It was customary for the owners of the best ponies to make them available to the players chosen to play for Shanghai. A gentle mount, Auburn had little speed, and most ponies could overtake him when play continued for long in one direction. When play reversed, however, he would stop and turn in a flash with the lightest reining in, to lead others near him by several lengths.

Marine officers were offered associate membership in the clubs, among them the Columbia Country Club (American) and the Shanghai Club (British). The latter, with the longest private bar (120 feet) in the world, occupied one of the substantial stone buildings that lined the Bund. When the cruiser *Augusta*, flagship of the Asiatic Squadron, made her semi-annual visits, she usually moored in midstream opposite the Shanghai Club. Viewed from the large window of the bar at second-story level, she was a sight to make one's heart swell. An imaginary line extended from the length of the bar would have hit her amidships.

There was also the American Club downtown and the French Club, Cercle Sportif Francais, near the 3d Battalion billets where one could play dominoes in the bar lounge. On Sunday afternoons in winter there was a *thé dansant* in the ballroom, which had a suspended floor that seemed to bounce lightly as one moved across it. That first November the officers of the regiment gave a ball there to celebrate the Marine Corps birthday. The officers of a recently arrived battalion of Argyll and Sutherland Highlanders in their kilts and scarlet mess jackets were the sensation of the evening.

A guest night at the Argylls officers mess was memorable. After the toasts, the pipers entered to march round and round the table making a joyful noise with their curious instruments. The martial skirling concluded, the colonel would pour a generous drink of whisky (instead of the decanted port that passed from hand to hand around the table) for the pipe major, who would down it at a gulp.

There were many nightclubs, ranging from such places as Delmonte's, where one bought tickets to dance with attractive Russian girls, and which had gambling upstairs, to Mont Berg's Little Club opposite the race course on Bubbling Well Road. Well-known people sometimes patronized the latter club. Count Ciano, then Italian Consul General in Shanghai, and his wife, a daughter of Mussolini, brought guests there occasionally. Once Mont introduced me to Douglas Fairbanks (senior) who was spending an evening ashore from a cruise ship.

Mont, who made no secret of having spent three years in San Quentin prison, always had a good floor show. He replaced his talent frequently,

The Color Guard of the 4th Marines with the band in the background, passing in review at a parade at the Race Course, Shanghai, during the 1930s. Courtesy U.S. Marine Corps.

The U.S.S. *Augusta*, flagship of the Asiatic Fleet, in the Whangpoo river, with a Yangtze River Patrol gunboat alongside. Picture taken from the Bund. Courtesy U.S. Naval Historical Center.

"Eyes right!" A platoon passing the reviewing stand during regimental parade at the Race Course, Shanghai, in the 1930s. The uniform is summer service khaki without the coat, at that time the warm-weather field uniform. Courtesy U.S. Marine Corps Museum.

The Legation Guard leaving for a winter field exercise, 1935, through what appears to be the Tung Pien Men or Eastern Convenience Gate. Courtesy Virginia Cheatham Van Ness.

but Nora Holt was a fixture during those years. A handsome, red-haired octaroon of mature years, she would belt out in her strong soprano old favorites like "Stormy Weather," or "The Man on the Flying Trapeze" (He floats through the air with the greatest of ease), or "Edie was a lady" (Though her past was shady).

At the Little Club I saw "Chesty" Puller for the first time in 1934 when the U.S.S. *Augusta* was moored off the Bund. A captain commanding the *Augusta*'s marine guard, he came in one evening with some naval officers after an official function. He had a Navy Cross from Nicaragua and would be awarded four more. With his ramrod-straight torso in the old high-collar white mess jacket, he was the center of attention as he strode across the tiny dance floor to a table.

After a year one could request transfer to the Legation Guard in Peking and experience a different aspect of China. The ambiance of that city was one of ancient culture and diplomacy rather than commerce. My friends 1st Lieutenant Peter* and Virginia Van Ness transferred to Peking but I was content in Shanghai. There were a number of unmarried young businessmen there. It was the custom for three or four of them to form a "mess" by renting a partially furnished apartment together and using the Peking rugs, china, and linen they were accumulating to take back home. They would hire a "number one boy" (chief steward) who would recruit a staff of at least three more servants. There had to be a cook, who might have a coolie to perform the more burdensome tasks and keep the kitchen spotless, and perhaps a "maky learn," who for a pittance was learning to prepare the strange dishes that foreigners demanded. The cook was supreme in his kitchen which he seldom left. Number one entered the kitchen only to pass through it to the servants area or for rather formal discussions with the cook regarding menus, marketing, and other details of feeding their employers.

Number one would have as many houseboys under him as the household required. They performed all household work other than that done in the kitchen, acted as valets, and waited on table. Servants addressed their employers as Master and Missy. As a rule, Chinese servants, except amahs (children's nurses) did not live in. They arrived well before the family's hour of rising to draw baths, waken their employers with a cup of tea or a glass of orange juice, and prepare breakfast. Luncheon, referred to as "tiffin" by foreigners in China, was a substantial meal. The dinner hour was late, about eight or eight-thirty. There were many dinner parties in the International Settlement. Sometimes the host's china and silver would be insufficient for the number of guests invited. When this happened,

---

*Colonel Cornelius Peter Van Ness, USMC, 1908–1953.

53

Household servants of Lt. and Mrs. C.P. Van Ness, 1934–35. From the left: Wash Amah, Rickshaw Boy, Cook, House Coolie, Number One, and "Small Boy." Foreigners in Peking usually had more servants than in Shanghai. In the latter, a chauffeur had replaced the rickshaw boy although there were hundreds of licensed rickshaws. Courtesy Virginia Cheatham Van Ness.

This substantial Shanghai residence was leased to the Marine Corps, serving as the regimental hospital, 4th Marines.

The 38th (Machine-Gun) Company, commanded by Captain John W. Thomason, Jr., of the Legation Guard in Peking in the early 1930s. At the upper right, overlooking the compound, is the gate tower known as Ch'ien Men. Captain Thomason, who successfully combined the two careers of professional soldier and author, is seen at the left wearing riding boots. The uniform is winter service green, equipped for the field. Winter service green with overcoats and the old 1918 steel helmet were the cold-weather field uniform before the Second World War.

Number one would informally borrow what was required from his counterparts in other households. Consequently, on some occasions guests were amused to find themselves using their own knives and forks when dining at the house of friends whose guest list had grown too large. Number one acquainted his mistress with the fact that dinner was ready with the simple announcement, "chow now, Missy."

Chinese servants came to work every day except Chinese New Year's Day, or on the day of the funeral of a close relative. Although they had two or three idle hours each afternoon and their employers dined out frequently, one long working day followed another. Loyal and utterly trustworthy despite their poverty and insecurity, they took their "cum-shaw" (kickback), a custom of the country. Most transactions, even drinks at a nightclub, were on credit. One signed a chit. On the day of reckoning for household bills the cook would receive a small rebate from the butcher and grocer.

In 1933, Bobby Denig, Paul Sherman,* and I obtained permission to quit the bachelor officer quarters to form such a mess. We rented a partly

*Brigadier General Paul D. Sherman, USMC (Ret).

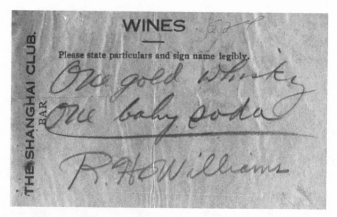

One seldom paid cash for anything on the China Coast. Chits were totaled and billed at the end of the month, sometimes even longer intervals. The sums were "Mex." In 1932, the Chinese dollar was about five for one U.S. dollar. Small coins were purchased at the clubs to pay rickshaw boys.

furnished two-bedroom apartment in the French Concession, where we lived amicably and well. Although the pay and allowances of a lieutenant were modest, the combined resources of three compared favorably with the pay of a lieutenant colonel of twenty-five years service. Indeed, we boldly invited two lieutenant colonels (our battalion commanders) and their wives to dine formally with us one evening. This black-tie occasion enabled us to display our taste in rugs and, we hoped, to create a favorable impression with the food and wine we served and the variety of liqueurs and old brandy we offered with coffee.

V

INTERNATIONAL POLO
AT ICHANG

Many officers of the 4th Marines visited North China and Japan but I hoarded my leave. I did, however, spend many weeks on one of the great rivers of the world. The Yangtze Kiang flows 3,100 miles generally east from its source in the highlands of Tibet to empty into the East China Sea near Shanghai. There were no bridges across the Yangtze, which was navigable for only its last 1,400 miles below Chungking. At Wahnsien, 150 miles downriver from Chungking, the Yangtze begins to flow through 200 miles of gorges. This is the upper river which drops from an elevation of 650 feet at Chungking to 130 feet at Ichang, whence it continues in more leisurely fashion another 1,000 miles to the ocean. Hard rock ledges in the bed of the upper river and falling rock from the canyon walls cause treacherous rapids at low water. With the spring rains, the upper river could rise more than 100 feet in the gorges, causing sustained high water in the middle and lower river basins.

During the high water of summer, seagoing ships of 10,000 tons could steam all the way up the lower river to Hankow, a busy port with many European residents and some Americans. From there, river craft of 4,000 tons could traverse the entire middle river to Ichang. The middle river meandered unpredictably over a flood plain during the high water of summer. Ships would get lost by turning out of the channel and cruising over what was countryside during low water.

Only the 1,000-ton motor vessels of the Yangtze Rapids Steamship Company, an American firm, could negotiate the upper river. They could do so in both summer and winter, during high and low water. Fitted with triple rudders to cope with sharp bends when racing down river, and with engines powerful enough to make headway against a 14-knot current over rapids when heading upstream, these craft shuttled cargo between

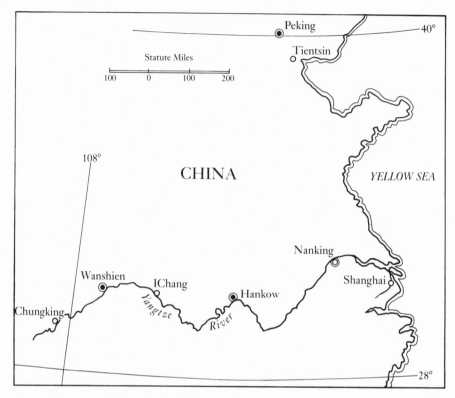

The Yangtze River and portion of the east coast of China.

Chungking and the transshipping port of Ichang, periodically returning to Shanghai to refit.

Beginning in 1933, after two or three of these vessels were fired upon from the river banks by bandits or some of Chairman Mao's Communist soldiers of the Long March then in progress, the regiment provided armed guards, consisting of a lieutenant and four marines. It was "good duty," as marines used to refer to any duty that was undemanding, watching rural China glide by from the deck of a riverboat. My first assignment to this duty was to the *I-An* which was to return to the upper river after refitting in Shanghai. My marines as well as I were assigned staterooms on the main deck of the little motor vessel.

One marine was on watch during the day, two at night. Underway I took the afternoon watch myself so the guard could enjoy a four-handed game of cards. Meals were good and we were not charged for them. I messed with the captain, a cheerful Irish-American named Avery who was known as the Duke of Ireland. During the trip I finished *Anthony Adverse*, a very long best-seller of the period.

This picture of the Horse Lung and Ox Hive Gorge on the Yangtze River gives some idea of the depth of the gorges. Note the unidentified steamboat which is probably a Yangtze River Steamship Co. motor vessel. Courtesy Naval Photographic Center.

Between Ichang and Chungking (the Upper River) the Yangtze flows for 200 miles through deep gorges. This picture of the Hung Lin Tan Rapid gives some idea of the hazards encountered by the motor vessels of the Yangtze Rapids Steamship Company when struggling upstream against a fast current or racing downstream riding one. Courtesy U.S. Naval Historical Center.

The U.S.S. *Palos*, with H.M.S. *Gannett* in background at Chungking in 1935. Both are "dressed overall" for some occasion. Courtesy of the late VAdm T.G.W. Settle U.S.N. (Ret), who was then, as a lieutenant commander, captain of the *Palos*.

In summer a few foreigners might take a holiday cruise on the Yangtze, but none did so in winter. The other staterooms were empty, but the deck below near the waterline was crowded with Chinese. At evening on the upper river when the vessel moored, the sickly sweet odor of opium burning in many pipes wafted up. Although the masters, usually Americans, were competent deepwater men, they yielded the bridge to a Chinese pilot on the upper river. The pilot's eyes seemed never to leave the water as he gave frequent signals to the helmsman with the fingers of one hand which rested on the sill of the wheelhouse window. Nothing moved on the upper river at night.

From 1854 until the outbreak of war with Japan in 1941, the U.S. Navy maintained the Yangtze River Patrol. These coal-burning gunboats patrolled only the lower and middle rivers, although there was a gunboat, the *Palos*, at Chungking. Because she needed help to get over some of the rapids, it took her thirteen days to get from Ichang to Chungking, a four-day trip for a motor vessel. She remained there showing the flag for

60

two years, functioning more like an outpost fort in frontier country than a patrol boat.

When a river port below the gorges was menaced by the approach of bandits or the troops of a warlord not in the service of Nanking, one or two gunboats would proceed to the threatened locality, prepared to take U.S. nationals on board and evacuate them to safety. Usually the mere presence of the gunboats, serenely riding at anchor in the stream, was enough to prevent any trouble. During the middle 1930s, there was little excitement on the Yangtze. In 1937, the Japanese attacked and sank the U.S. gunboat *Panay*, but that occurred after my return to the United States.

Many dull days were passed at anchor or alongside a float. The officers and crew of a gunboat stationed at one of the smaller river ports for some time often devised ingenious forms of amusement. I discovered this when, after finally being promoted to first lieutenant in 1934, I took another armed guard upriver in December on board the motor vessel *I-Ping*, having volunteered to spend the holidays away from Shanghai in order to save money.

One Saturday in December, the *I-Ping* (in which Peter Van Ness had earlier taken an armed guard and Virginia had accompanied him as a passenger) anchored near the company warehouse at Ichang as sampans swarmed about her sides. The gunboat *Monocacy* was tied up at the Standard Oil float below the town. I was directed to report on board any gunboat encountered, if practicable, so I got into a sampan and succeeded in making the boatman understand that I wished to be taken to the *Monocacy*. A small sampan was propelled, rather than rowed, by its owner. Instead of sitting on a thwart facing the stern and pulling two oars with long strokes, a Chinese riverman stands in the bow and pushes a single oar with rapid short strokes.

Gunboats were scow-like, of light draft, captained by a lieutenant commander, with a crew of forty or fifty. I was welcomed aboard as one coming from civilization and taken ashore for a drink. Accepting the invitation to dine in the tiny wardroom, I passed on the news and gossip of Shanghai. As we lingered over coffee, the executive officer turned to a junior grade lieutenant.

"How about the polo sticks?"

"The carpenter will have them ready by noon tomorrow, Sir." Then, turning to me, "do you know anything about polo?" Bewildered, I admitted to some knowledge of the game. I had played a little at Kiangwan before the economies of the Depression had forced the regiment to sell the ponies. The fact that I had played caused mild excitement. Everyone spoke at once. I gathered that they wanted me to play on their side on Sunday in a match with the three officers of a little British gunboat,

An earlier armed guard on board the *I'Ping* under command of the First Lt. C.P. Van Ness, center. Courtesy Virginia Cheatham Van Ness. Mrs. Van Ness accompanied her husband as a passenger. Many Shanghai residents made vacation trips in the Yangtze Rapids Steamship Company's motor vessels to see the gorges and the river ports.

The U.S.S. *Monocacy* at Nanking in 1932. Courtesy Commander Robert L. Mitlen.

H.M.S. *Gannet*. Since the *I-Ping* was to remain at Ichang for two days taking on cargo for Chungking, I said I was willing to play but had no riding gear with me.

"Oh, you won't need any," said the executive officer. "The *Gannet* is anchored 400 yards below us. You may have noticed her. Challenged us yesterday. They supply the ponies and we provide the sticks. Game is at 1430. None of us know anything about polo, so if you've played at all, you will be a great help."

This further confused rather than clarified the situation for me. "But where do you obtain polo ponies way up here?" I asked.

"I don't know where the limeys found them. I'm sure they've never played polo, but neither have we. The ship's carpenter is making enough sticks for both sides."

"Out of what?" I asked. The executive officer looked at me.

"Wood," he said briefly.

"And the ball?" I asked in a subdued voice.

"Well, you see, we're going to play on the Limey soccer field. It's up above, on the bluff near the club where we went for cocktails before dinner. We thought we could use an American recreation baseball, an old one that is fairly soft, and play indoor polo rules with three on a side. The *Gannet* has only three officers including the captain who has played some polo before. If you play, the two sides should be about evenly matched in goal ratings."

I sent back to the *I-Ping* for a few things with a note to the corporal of my guard explaining the turn of events, and stayed the night in the gunboat. After tiffin on Sunday the *Gannet*'s motor sampan came alongside with the challenging team. I was introduced and my presence explained.

The captain of the *Gannett* asked if we were ready to play and explained that they had obtained ponies after a bit of bargaining on the surgeon's part. In fact, he went on, pointing to the top of the bluff, the bloody little beasts were just arriving. Looking up we could see a procession of undersized, long-haired ponies, saddled and bridled, moving along the path near the edge of the bluff toward the football field.

"Oh, yes. We hadn't forgotten the sticks?" they queried. The captain of the *Monocacy* looked questioningly at his lieutenant, junior grade, who appeared a little worried.

"Yes, Sir. And a few extra in case any get broken. They're odd-looking, though. Heavy on the hitting end. I thought I had made it clear to the carpenter's mate what we wanted, but apparently he thought you hit the ball with the end of the mallet. I didn't find out until he had about finished them. They look like croquet mallets."

To the obvious relief of the j.g. everyone laughed. We saw what he meant, though, when two mess boys fetched the sticks. They were rather formidable-looking, rough-hewn cylinders, fashioned from some kind of soft wood with a length of bamboo stuck into a hole in the middle.

"Who is going to umpire?" asked our captain, in whose place I was to play.

"Oh, our soldier," replied the captain of H.M.S. *Gannet*. "He is already up on the field." A subaltern of the Royal Inniskilling Fusiliers, who had succeeded the Argylls in Shanghai, had also arrived the previous evening. I knew him slightly. His unit provided armed guards for British merchant ships on the middle river. We stepped ashore to climb the steps to the soccer field keyed up for some rare fun: international polo at Ichang—the U.S. Navy vs. the Royal Navy.

When I saw the ponies at close range, however, I had misgivings. The China pony with which I was familiar in Shanghai was a stout little fellow of about 12½ hands. Tireless, he had a great heart and never succumbed to men's ways after running free on the Mongolian Plain for several years. These little fellows were not Mongolian, but Szechuan ponies. The largest might have reached 11 hands! When ground rules were agreed upon, play began. It was not polo, of course.

The diminutive creatures were bewildered, terrified by the swinging mallets, the wild shouts, and the strange evolutions their awkward riders tried to put them through, but it was a riot of fun for players and spectators. The former were terribly in earnest, whacking their reluctant mounts on the crupper to startle them into plunging jerkily forward. The ponies refused to canter, so the match was played at a trot. Often, just as a player was in the lead and riding hard for a ball in the open, poised for a terrific wallop for goal, his pony would stop dead six feet from the ball, and one of Uncle Sam's or His Majesty's naval officers would hit the deck.

Although the Szechuan ponies were small and a fall from one was not dangerous, it was no less an indignity. Perhaps the spectators enjoyed this aspect of the match most. The crews of both ships were there, the petty officers of both services forming a little group to themselves. My marines were there too, and the Chinese were represented by the *mafoos** and a number of others who came to see what foolishness the hairy foreign devils were up to this time.

The lieutenant of the Royal Inniskilling Fusiliers umpired the game on foot. He called no fouls but was kept busy retrieving the ball and throwing it back into play. Somehow goals were made. At the end of the third chukker it was apparent that sticks, ponies, and players would be

*Chinese stable boys.

Polo played on China ponies was a popular pastime for marine officers in Peking and Shanghai. These Peking marines seem to be having a great time trying to play the game on what appear to be very small donkeys, whacking a volley ball with brooms. Courtesy U.S. Marine Corps Museum.

good for only one more. The score was tied at five all, and the ponies were tired and unwilling as we rode out for the last chukker. The heads had parted from several mallets. One player on each side had only a bamboo stick with which to poke at the ball. The contest became a yelling, pushing scrum in which the ball was seldom hit. The Scottish medical officer accidentally struck our executive officer a smart blow on the head. Fortunately he was the only player on the field who wore a sun helmet.

Time was nearly up when our j.g., who had scarcely laid a stick on the ball all afternoon, leaned over and lofted it in a beautiful arc to within ten feet of the Royal Navy's goal posts. All six players charged down the field like cavalry, riding knee to knee at a fast trot. No one could swing at the ball. Spectators were yelling and running down the field with us. We rode on to the ball, over it, and on past the goal line. As we struggled to turn our ponies around, a great shout arose from the American side of the field. One of the little brutes had kicked the ball between the uprights.

Afterward we all went aboard the *Gannet* for drinks. Unlike the U.S. Navy, the wine mess was as much a part of a British naval vessel as the rudder. The following morning the *I-Ping* got underway about 1100 and by lunchtime we were entering the great gorges of the upper Yangtze.

I spent the next few weeks shuttling between Ichang and Chungking. Toward the end of January 1935 I received a radio message via the

Yangtze River Patrol to transfer to a middle river boat bound for Shanghai. Ten days later, one morning after a late arrival, I reported to regimental headquarters on Haiphong Road. Captain Pat Kelly, the adjutant, greeted me warmly.

"Do sit down. Well, now" he said in his rich voice with a trace of brogue, "who is it that you know in Washington?" Lifting a document from his hold basket he began to quote excerpts:
From: The Major General Commandant
To: First Lieutenant Robert H. Williams, USMC
Subject: Permanent Change of Station

1. On or about 20 February 1935 . . . you will stand detached from your present station and duties and proceed to Marine Barracks, Quantico, Virginia . . . authorized three months delay in reporting to count as leave . . . plus 55 days travel time . . . authorized to proceed via Europe utilizing commercial transportation either via the Suez Canal or the Trans-Siberian Railway . . . authorized to claim reimbursement equal to what it would cost the Government to order you via first class commercial transportation from Shanghai to Seattle, and by rail across the continent at eight cents a mile . . . authorized by the Secretary of the Navy to draw three months pay in advance . . . .

"In all my years in the Marine Corps," said Pat, "I've never seen orders like these. Who is your friend at court?"

"I don't know anyone at headquarters, Sir. I've never been to Washington." I thought of my benefactor at headquarters, but he was no longer on duty there.

"Then how do you explain these orders?"

"Well, Sir. I requested them—well, not everything, of course. I didn't ask for Quantico—just the East Coast—and I didn't ask to go via Russia."

"Oh, you requested them," Pat gently mimicked me. "That, of course, explains it. And when did you put in your request?"

"About six months ago, Sir. There was something about it in a headquarters circular letter."

"I think I remember it. Must have been a year ago. Orderly!"

A well-turned-out private first class marched in to halt smartly with a good heel click before the adjutant's desk. "Ask the sergeant major or one of his clerks for the circular letters for the first six months of 1934. Got that?"

"Aye, aye, Sir." The orderly performed a faultless about-face. After two minutes he returned with the circulars, and Pat began skimming through the file.

"Well I'll be damned," he muttered. Again he quoted:
The Detail Office frequently disapproves requests of officers for delay

to count as leave in excess of the 30 days customarily authorized in travel orders involving a permanent change of station. Similarly, requests of officers serving in the Far East to return via Europe are disapproved when such requests are received after original orders have been issued.

Officers who desire additional leave and permission to return via Europe from the Far East should address requests to the Major General Commandant six months before the end of the normal tour of duty. It may not be practicable to approve such requests but they will be given consideration.

"Well," said Pat, smiling again. "I expect the detail office will be receiving more such requests from this regiment from now on." With a gesture for me to remain seated, he rose, circular letter in hand, to pass through the louvered swinging door to the adjacent office of the regimental commander, Colonel John C. Beaumont. Pat soon reappeared in the doorway, beckoning to me. Johnny Beau, handsome and urbane, congratulated me on my orders, and remarked that he would like to be a lieutenant again for six weeks so he could take an armed guard upriver.

VI

FULL CIRCLE

I left Shanghai on 26 February 1935 in the Dollar Line's *President Van Buren*, a cabin-class ship that carried cargo out of Seattle, on a round-the-world cruise. I boarded the ship with only $15 in my wallet and a token balance in a drawing account in the First National Bank of Quantico, Virginia. With the money I had saved while upriver, I had paid for my Peking rugs and other purchases, including a set of Thousand Flower china for eight that I could not resist buying in Kunming. The $600 "dead horse" (three months pay in advance) had been used to pay for my steamship ticket to Marseilles and a rail ticket to Paris. Special arrangements were necessary to obtain more money for the incidental expenses of travel, for a stay of several weeks in Europe, and for passage across the Atlantic. I had written to my father immediately upon receiving my orders asking him to cable $200 to the Chase Bank in Manila. The letter departed the same day on an Empress liner due in Seattle seventeen days later, then the fastest scheduled crossing of the Pacific. I also obtained a blank note on the Quantico bank from a brother officer, which Bobby Denig and Paul Sherman co-signed for $500. I then mailed this with instructions to the bank to send the draft to American Express, Paris.

Much of the business of the Quantico bank's loan department was with bachelor lieutenants who cheerfully co-signed each others' notes for $200 or $300 on a monthly allotment repayment plan. The bank was risking little because no officer was apt to mar his service reputation by ignoring his debts. It was a convenience to be able to raise money in this way. Five hundred dollars, however, was more than the usual amount requested. I could not be certain that the loan would be granted but I had no collateral in any case. With the confidence of youth, however, I considered that I had sufficiently provided for the continuation of my trip around the world and forgot about it.

The *President Van Buren* was berthed across the Whangpoo, opposite the Bund. Bobby Denig came to see me off. I had my trunks taken aboard but remained on the quay although the ship was ready for sea and passengers were back on board. We sat on a bench, talking idly of past events and things to come. He hoped to marry little Mary Drake, an American who had been brought up in Shanghai. She had recently moved with her parents to Hong Kong.

Something reminded us of our breakfast visit a year earlier to the 1st Battalion mess hall. We were acting as judges for the monthly award of the regimental mess pennant. Each of the three judges made an unannounced visit, usually separately, to each mess hall three times each month to take breakfast, and a noon and evening meal. Bobby and I, however, sampled breakfast together at the 1st Battalion general mess in unusual circumstances.

We had been toying with a last whisky and soda, unwanted really, at Delmonte's, which was about to close. Only two couples were dancing. The pretty Russian girls at their tables on one side of the dance floor were clutching their evening bags in anticipation of the orchestra's breaking into "Good Night Sweetheart" when they would rise in a body and go home. Though still dark outside, marines would already be rising in their billets on this wintry morning.

We had arrived at Delmonte's quite late, not having left the Saint Patrick's Day Ball at the French Club until after the music stopped at 0300. It was the custom of foreign patriotic societies to give balls on the days of tribal observance, and we had been detailed, not unwillingly, to attend. There was also a Saint George's Ball, a Caledonian Ball, and an American Ball. The latter took place on Washington's Birthday rather than Independence Day because on Bastille Day, July fourteenth, the French Club gave a magnificent celebration. The invitation to the commanding officer of the 4th Marines to attend with several of his officers always requested that he and his officers be in uniform. We were still in evening dress uniform as our pleasant evening of dancing and drinking came to an end in the early hours of the morning.

"Heh," said Denig. "I'm hungry. It's time for breakfast. Have you had breakfast at the 1st Battalion yet this month?"

"No."

"Well, let's go. For a mess hall, mess jackets should be appropriate." We signed our chits and found a taxi outside. The end of the line was being served as we entered a bare, dimly lit mess hall. Marines uniformed in green kersey sat at benches fixed to both sides of long tables on either side of a center aisle, wolfing down a hearty breakfast. We were wrapped in dark boat cloaks which almost reached the floor. Because of the damp chill, we had not thrown the right side of our cloaks back over the right shoulder to reveal the scarlet lining and thus were scarcely noticed at first. I asked a passing messman to tell the mess sergeant that he had visitors.

We had uncovered as we entered as was customary and now removed our boat cloaks. The mess sergeant hurried toward us, pop-eyed at the sight of these two splendidly uniformed second lieutenants. We introduced ourselves as regimental mess judges wishing to take breakfast and have a look around the galley. We were conscious that the mess hall clamor was dying down to be replaced by a questioning silence. Knives and forks were suspended in the air as the breakfasters, their elbows on the table, paused to stare. "Who are them people?" I heard a young marine ask wonderingly as the mess sergeant led us to a small table with a single place setting.

"Sir, the OD had a cup of coffee in the galley and left," he informed us. "He won't be eating breakfast. I'll have another place set." We had not realized that we should be making such a spectacle. It occurred to me that few of those marines had ever seen an officer in a mess jacket, a striking garment that attracted attention even among other dress uniforms. It was of a midnight blue that was blacker than black in artificial light. The high-waisted, pocketless trousers had stripes of gold enriched by thin lines of scarlet from waist to ankle. The jacket was short, waist high in back, with the open front fastened only at the base of the high, gold-embroidered, standing collar which was in the style of the earlier years of the nineteenth century. The jacket front was cut to fall away to the waist, increasingly exposing the starched and gold-studded shirtbosom and white piqué vest. From the right side of the collar to the bottom of the jacket ran a line of sixteen small gold buttons. Opposite them were false buttonholes which, had they been real, could not possibly have fastened the buttons. An unpointed, standing shirt collar was concealed by the jacket collar except at the throat where the loop (which alone fastened the jacket) overlaid it and the barely visible knot of the black bow tie. Removable knots of twisted gold coils bearing the globe and anchor and insignia of rank were attached to the jacket shoulders, the sleeves of which were heavy with broad soutaches of gold braid. There was but one pocket, inside the right breast, in which one could put a thin wallet and a small cigarette case. A handkerchief was stuffed up a sleeve.

The marines soon resumed eating their breakfast, for they had no time to waste. There were the usual chores to be done to get their quarters ready for inspection before turning out to stand morning colors. We finished our meal and left after a brief look at the galley and words of thanks and appreciation to the mess sergeant and chief cook. It was time to return to our own quarters, to get out of our finery, to bathe and shave and put on the uniform of the day. Sleep had to be deferred until after lunch .

Denig looked up. What he saw quickly brought us back into the present. "Get going," he said, "or you'll miss your ship." I leapt to my feet, gave him a farewell punch in the chest, and took off at a run as the stern of the *President Van Buren* was slowly moving away from the quay. Racing up the steps of the high platform which the dock hands were about to remove, I reached the level of the main deck and jumped aboard, much to the merriment of a number of passengers.

I had come to the end of a chapter. As the ship started downstream I could make out the Shanghai Club. One year I had attended the Autumn Ball there, a white-tie occasion and the only time during the year when ladies were admitted to the club. It was a custom at this ball that sometime during a dance intermission each lady be hoisted up to sit on the famous bar to drink a glass of champagne.

I could locate Sir Victor Sassoon's Cathay Hotel as we passed Nanking Road. It had a lounge on the sixth floor which offered dining and dancing nightly. I recalled how a scavenger hunt had ended there one evening in a riot of fun. Phil Carpenter,* Bobby Denig, and I had sent our invitations for a mysterious party to a dozen couples, twelve young men whom we had carefully paired with twelve girls. Most of them were Americans, none was married, and all were in their early twenties. It began with a black-tie dinner at the officers' club. Over coffee and liqueurs at 2115 we revealed our plans for the remainder of the evening by providing our guests with typed instructions. These set forth six or seven tasks for each pair to accomplish in any order between 2130 and 2345, when they must report to us at the Cathay Hotel with proof of accomplishment. One was a platform ticket from North Station, miles across town, another a bar chit for a Tom and Jerry at the Metropole Hotel bar. The last was to be something alive, not a dog or a cat, which they had to bring with them. It would be judged for originality and would be the basis for selecting the winning couple from among those who had completed all the tasks within the alloted time.

It was better than a floor show for the other people who had taken tables on the sixth floor that evening. We had reserved a long table near the dance floor for our party, but the judging took place near the elevators from which burst couple after couple as the hands of the clock approached midnight. They clutched or dragged after them many forms of life—a Russian taxi dancer, a Sikh policeman, chickens, ducks, doves, a huge

*The late Phillip S.P. Carpenter of Philadelphia.

green parrot, and a man with a gibbon—but the winner was an ancient Chinese chestnut vendor, his equipment balanced on a *hei ho* pole with chestnuts steaming. The *North China Daily News* had rushed a reporter to the scene.

Sadness gripped me briefly as I gazed on the city for the last time on that February day in 1935. I had no presentiment then that the regiment would soon suffer defeat under General MacArthur, and captivity under General Wainwright in the Philippines, as the Western way of life on the China Coast receded abruptly into history. Standing on deck among other passengers, yet feeling isolated and alone, I felt a hand on my shoulder and turned to recognize a U.S. Navy lieutenant whom I had met a month earlier on my way downriver. He had also received travel orders home with permission to go via the Suez Canal.

I had two $1 bills in my wallet when I got off the ship at Manila. Although there had not been time for a letter from my father to reach me, the $200 awaited me at the Chase bank. It seemed an ample sum with which to travel to Paris. My only expenses would be at the ship's bar, tips for stewards, laundry, and sightseeing ashore.

Most passengers left the ship at Singapore to stay two nights at Raffles Hotel. There I researched the Singapore Gin Sling,* then a popular afternoon drink in warm weather. Recipes varied. People argued about how it should be mixed but it seemed logical that the correct one would be found at Raffles. A former British cavalry officer learned that I hoped to be in London for the Silver Jubilee and advised me to book a room without delay.

"Everyone in the British Isles who can manage it will be in London then," he said. "Should be a good show. Don't miss it. I'll post a note to a small private hotel I know of in Kensington asking them to book a room for you. Let's exchange cards. I'll put the address on mine for you. Princess Gate. Put the date of your arrival in London and length of stay on the back of yours."

The Navy lieutenant and I shared a room at Raffles, but he had only thirty days delay and did not plan to visit England. Our cavalryman introduced us to the engineer in residence at the naval base which was then in an early stage of construction. British people seem better able to accept Americans when meeting them abroad. They put aside their reserve sooner and display an easy friendliness.

The engineer said that it was rather lonely out there for him and his wife. The children were in school at home. The bungalow was comfortable enough, but their nearest neighbor was miles away. How long was

---

*My researches determined that the recipe required a jigger of Cherry Herring brandy in addition to the gin, a bit of lemon peel finely grated, and a teaspoon of grenadine.

our ship to be in port? Wouldn't we like to drive out tomorrow morning? It really wasn't far. Pamela would be delighted. It would break the monotony for her and there would be curry for tiffin. That is, if we liked curry? Indeed we did! The following morning this friendly Englishman, whose earth-moving machinery consisted of 1,500 coolies, showed us extensive excavations where concrete had been poured for underground generators and two immense graving docks.

Only Japan posed a threat to the Royal Navy in those waters. When war came only a few years later the Singapore Naval Base would be operational, but to no one had it occurred that the Japanese Army might come swarming down the Malay Peninsula to overrun the city and the base with dismaying ease.

On that March day of 1935, when thirst and the mid-day sun forced us into the cool gloom of the airy tropical bungalow, the Japanese threat to Britain's hegemony in Southeast Asia seemed remote. Our hostess was attractive. The curried chicken, hot and spicy, was served superbly by four native servants. For them the offering of gourmet fare on gleaming silver for guests to transfer to the fairest china was as the parade is to the soldier.

At Bombay the port authority required all passengers to move ashore. We stayed at the Taj Mahal, another of those substantial hotels built around an open court designed to invite even the slightest breeze. Staffed with polite, brown-skinned little men and provided with spacious bed-rooms cooled by four-bladed fans attached to the high ceilings, they offered food and drink and shelter to the grateful traveler in the tropical belt the world over, before the day of air conditioning.

Following our stay in Bombay, there were many days on the water as the ship steamed through the Arabian Sea into the Gulf of Aden and up the long Red Sea. On those quiet evenings we lingered on the boat deck, enchanted by the afterglow of the sunset over Africa as the moon arose over Arabia. At Suez the Navy lieutenant and I left the ship with two Canadian girls, sisters who were taking the entire cruise, to motor over the desert to Cairo, where we spent three days before rejoining the ship at Alexandria.

Our companions stayed at the old Shepheards's Hotel, with whose stately charm we became familiar. The Navy lieutenant and I, mindful of coming expenses in Europe, stayed at a less distinguished hotel nearby. Finally, after a stop at Naples and a visit to Pompeii, where we left the Navy lieutenant who wished to see something of Italy, I disembarked at Marseilles and boarded a night train for Paris.

After unpacking in my little room at the Petit Royal, a respectable small hotel on the Left Bank around a corner from the Cafe de Dome, I sought the sunny streets and purchased a map. Again there were only two $1 bills in my wallet. With only a few francs in my pocket I boarded a bus instead of taking a taxi for the Place de l'Opera, but the $500 draft from the Quantico bank was waiting for me at the American Express office. I enquired about Baltimore Mail Line departures. The small ships of that line took nine days to cross from Le Havre to Norfolk, but the single-class fare was only $110.

I prudently booked passage home toward the end of May and paid for it before walking over to the box office of the Opera. A pleasant French woman sold me a box seat for a performance of *Le Chevalier à la Rose* after having cautioned me that it was a dress night and received my assurance of compliance. I also obtained an orchestra seat in the center of the house for another evening. Recalling Lon Chaney in the *Phantom of the Opera*, I took a fancy to sit under the great chandelier that figured so largely in that film. When I took my seat for the second performance, a plumb line, if lowered from its center, would have rested on my head. Quite satisfied with my first morning in Paris I sat down at a sidewalk table at the Cafe de la Paix, ordered an aperitif, and broke out my map.

Early in May I left Paris for London to stay at the modest private hotel (in America it would have been called a boarding house) in Kensington where the ex-cavalryman in Singapore had booked a room for me. London during a brilliant season seemed even more wonderful than Paris. On Monday morning 6 May 1935 I took the underground (subway) to Trafalgar Square to watch the royal procession from Buckingham Palace to Saint Paul's on the silver anniversary of the accession of King George V to the throne. Several of the royal family groups rode past in open carriages to polite applause, but wave after wave of cheers from tens of thousands of throats rolled on ahead to herald the approach of Edward, Prince of Wales. Wearing the uniform of the colonel of the Welsh Guards, the prince kept his right hand almost continuously at the salute. His tall black bearskin bobbed from side to side as he turned right and left to make little bows of acknowledgement. At the end came the monarch and his queen behind six greys with a sovereign's escort of the household cavalry.

After a few days in Wales I recrossed the Channel to embark in the *City of Norfolk*. Little of the $500 remained. One afternoon in mid-ocean word passed that a big ship could be seen off the starboard quarter. It seemed strange that a ship bound for New York was in the same sea lane as ours, but there was the *Aquitania*. Rapidly overtaking us, she passed at about 1,200 yards to disappear into the mist and low ceiling. It was a little depressing. The great liner, which would cross the ocean in less than five days, had overtaken us so quickly that it seemed as though our little vessel was making sternway.

Toward the end of May the *City of Norfolk* docked at her namesake port. After tipping the stewards, I had less than $5 remaining in my wallet, so it was necessary to go to the marine barracks at the Naval Operating Base to see the paymaster before proceeding to Wisconsin to stay with my parents at their vacation home, "Bryn Mawr." Having just worked off my three months dead horse, I had little pay coming but would receive all my quarters and ration allowances (which one could not draw in advance) since February. The paymaster, an elderly captain, carefully read my orders with growing amazement, made his calculations, and paid me $300.

That afternoon I boarded a train for Chicago. In the club car before supper, I first experienced the change in America that resulted from the repeal of the Volstead Act—Prohibition had ended. My last drink in the United States had been mixed with bootleg whisky and consumed surreptitiously.

The Depression was still with us but not because of inactivity on the part of President Franklin D. Roosevelt and his New Deal. From the conversation of two businessmen, I gathered that many people of substance bitterly opposed the President, regarding him as a traitor to his class, but that the great mass of the people admired him and believed in him and his ability to govern. He had a common touch and could speak to them over the radio in terms they understood. He had surmounted what most men in his physical condition would have regarded as a hopeless handicap in seeking high office.

Later, as I lay in my berth, I reflected that the Corps had also changed significantly. It was 1935 and the day of gunboat diplomacy was over. Having trained constabularies in Haiti and Nicaragua during years of occupation, the marines had been withdrawn. This had made it possible for the Navy Department to authorize the reorganization of the East and West Coast Expeditionary Forces as the Fleet Marine Force. The FMF was a permanent landing force consisting initially of two very small brigades of combined arms with aviation support, directly under the commander in chief of the U.S. Fleet.

Paralleling the organization and training of the new fleet component was a change in the orientation of the Marine Corps Schools in Quantico. In addition to revising the curriculum to concentrate on the techniques of landing operations, they were developing a landing force doctrine. After having analyzed the British failure at Gallipoli in 1915 as a point of departure, the Schools' staff was preparing, in conjunction with the Naval

War College, a tentative landing operations manual to serve as guidance for the FMF.

A new phrase, "passed over for promotion," described what had happened to several captains and first lieutenants and one field officer of the 4th Marines in Shanghai the previous summer. In 1934, Congress had passed legislation which enabled the Marine Corps to adopt the selection board system in place of promotion by seniority alone. Boards were now convened each year by the Secretary of the Navy and directed to recommend a stated number of officers from among those with sufficient service in grade to be eligible for promotion to the next higher grade. The number of officers a board was directed to recommend was less than the total within the promotion zone that it was to consider. Thus boards were forced to pass over a number of officers whom they believed to be the least fit for advancement. Those passed over twice by successive boards were involuntarily transferred to the retired list. It was beginning to look as though the World War "hump" would disappear and a reasonable flow of promotion achieved through the company grades. I could look forward to becoming a captain within a few years.

After several weeks in Wisconsin, I returned east to report for duty. I still had some leave left but it was well to have some in reserve; four and a half months of leisure and travel had been enough. Upon my arrival in Norfolk my orders had been modified, and my new duty station was no longer Quantico. Instead I was directed to report to Marine Barracks, 8th and I Streets, Southeast, Washington, D.C.

Colonel Emile P. Moses was the commanding officer there. As a lieutenant colonel he had been the executive officer of the 4th Marines when I arrived in Shanghai in 1932. This was a welcome change. My orders to Quantico had not been to the Fleet Marine Force, but to the post where I should probably have received some dull administrative assignment. To be able to live in the nation's capital was much more attractive. Only a few officers during their entire careers ever served at the historic old Barracks, home of the U.S. Marine Band, where the Commandant's House was located.

A day or two after reporting, I changed into a white uniform after duty hours to pay the customary calls on the commanding officer and others along officers row. I think it was Mrs. Pearce, wife of the post quartermaster, who asked me something about New York City. "I don't know," I replied, "I've never been there."

"You've never been to New York?" She stared at me in hilarious disbelief. "Oh, how divine! But it can't be true! Why, you've been around the world and have just spent two months in Europe after a tour in China.

And you must have spent your first year after being commissioned at the Basic School in Philadelphia. It's simply incredible! Just wait until I tell some of my friends about you."

I finally got to New York before the year was out. Meanwhile, I must have been regarded as something of a curiosity because I received what seemed to me an unusual number of invitations to dinner. We had a saying in the *Old Corps*, "we don't get much money, but we have a lot of fun."

VII

THE BARRACKS

It used to confuse people that the Washington Navy Yard (for many years called the Naval Gun Factory when it served as such) had its own marine barracks. Now remodeled to house the Marine Corps Historical Center, the building that was the barracks from 1941 to 1975 is still there at the southeast corner of the sloping little parade ground. Eighth Street SE ends at what was formerly the principal entrance to the yard, Benjamin Latrobe's main gate completed in 1805. It is more than a gate. An archway the length of a house tunnels at street level through a three-story structure of mostly officers quarters which in the past were sometimes used for offices. It interrupts and rises above the sturdy wall of the yard along M Street. In 1935, the Navy Yard marines were quartered in the part of this building west of the archway. From the Latrobe Gate it is only a short walk up 8th Street to the oldest post of the Corps, Marine Barracks, 8th and I Streets, Southeast, Washington, D.C.

If you are visiting the Barracks, you will enter through a pair of wrought iron gates guarded by a sentry smartly turned out in blues. From there, if you continue straight on for about 100 feet, pause and face left, you will find yourself at one end of the parade ground within a walled compound of brick. To your back is the Band Hall with its raised arcade. Facing you at the other end of the parade ground is the Commandant's House, its gardens and side buildings together with the wall extending from corner to corner on G Street. The house is separated from the parade ground by a low iron fence and hedge. On your left along 8th Street, between the main gate and the garden of the Commandant's House, are five detached houses, officers' quarters that face the parade ground and are

79

The Latrobe Gate as seen from inside the Washington Navy Yard about 1942.
Before the Second World War, the Navy Yard marines were quartered in the part
of the structure to the left of the entrance from which 8th Street leads to Marine
Barracks, Washington, D.C. Courtesy U.S. Naval Historical Center.

The Commandant's House looking north from the parade ground.

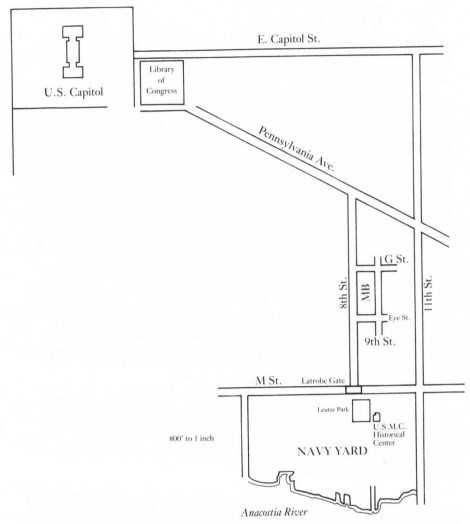

Map showing location of Navy Yard and Marine Barracks in Washington, D.C.

separated from it by a sidewalk and a row of trees. On your right, facing the officers' quarters across the parade ground, is a continuously arcaded structure. It contains offices and storerooms and formerly, at ground level, the general mess, with squad rooms for enlisted personnel on the second and partial third floors above. In 1975, a handsome quarters-mess-recreation complex for enlisted marines was completed on the south side of I Street, outside the original barracks to which it is connected by a tunnel.

Aerial view of Marine Barracks, Washington, D.C., in the 1930s. On the left (west) is 8th Street (note the street car) to the rear of five detached houses (married officers' quarters) facing the parade ground. The Commandant's House, first occupied in 1805, is at the far (north) end of the parade ground. The buildings on the right, next to 9th Street, comprised offices, store rooms, galley, and mess hall with enlisted quarters on the 2nd and 3rd floors. In the foreground, with its rear along I Street, is the band hall of the U.S. Marine Band. The main gate, not visible, is located on 8th Street between the left front of the band hall and quarters number five. Courtesy U.S. Marine Corps.

An officer who received orders to report for duty at Marine Barracks, Washington, D.C., realized that he was in a state of grace. The commanding officer and the commandant himself had consulted his fitness report file and made inquiries concerning his general service reputation and recent performance of duty. When I reported for duty in 1935, the complement of the post consisted of the Barracks Detachment, the Marine Corps Institute, and the U.S. Marine Band together with the Naval Examining Board for the promotion of officers, the Officer Candidate School, and the editorial office of the *Leatherneck*. All were administered by the usual post headquarters organization under Lieutenant Colonel Thomas S. Clarke, who had relieved Colonel Moses shortly after I reported. Colonel Clarke was a tall, portly officer in his middle fifties with a deliberate habit of mind, not given to hasty decisions.

The executive officer was Major Lemuel C. Shepherd, Jr., who one day would cap one of the most distinguished of Marine Corps careers by

Marine Barracks, Washington, D.C., in the 1930s. An arcade, above which were living quarters for enlisted marines, runs the length of the parade ground on the east side. A center walk cuts across the middle of the parade ground from the flagpole to quarters number three. Courtesy U.S. Marine Corps Museum.

becoming the twentieth commandant. A first classman at Virginia Military Institute when the United States declared war against Germany in April 1917, he saw the Barracks for the first time a few days later when he and several classmates came to Washington to be examined for their commissions. After passing brief oral and physical examinations, they were sworn in as second lieutenants in the Marine Corps Reserve. They then returned to VMI to complete their studies.

Lem Shepherd did not graduate with his class, however. The expanding Corps needed second lieutenants. At the commandant's request, he and his classmates who had been commissioned in the Reserve were graduated early. In May, he reported to the recruit training depot at Parris Island, South Carolina, where his schooling as an officer was interrupted by orders to proceed to Philadelphia and report to the 5th Regiment which was soon to sail for France. On the day in June when the Class of 1917 graduated at VMI, Second Lieutenant Shepherd was a platoon leader on board the naval transport *Henderson*, about to disembark at Saint Nazaire.

Two or three years before the selection system was introduced in 1934, Shepherd and other senior captains of the World War "hump" had been promoted to major under the old seniority system. He was to spend a relatively short time in the rank of major, however, for under the new selection system, he was promoted to lieutenant colonel a few weeks after I reported in 1935. It was something to talk about when Lieutenant

Colonel Shepherd was required to fire the range for record later that summer. Actually, he continued to do so voluntarily each year until he became a general officer, but at the time no one could recall a marine lieutenant colonel having to do so because he was not yet forty years of age.

There were no quarters for bachelor officers at the Barracks in 1935. The old Center House, which had stood on the 8th Street side opposite the flagpole since the earliest years of the post, had been torn down to make room for officers row when the Barracks underwent a major renovation in 1907. The house nearest the Main Gate, remodeled after the Second World War to become the Center House mess and quarters for bachelor officers, was assigned to a married officer, Captain Reginald H. Ridgely. Years of hardship and deprivation awaited him as a prisoner of war. He would be serving in the 4th Marines in 1941 when the regiment left Shanghai for the Philippines, shortly before the Japanese attack on Pearl Harbor, where it would suffer defeat.

When I reported for duty I lived at first in a hotel near Union Station until the officer I was to relieve as editor and publisher of the *Leatherneck* magazine, as well as assistant registrar of the Marine Corps Institute, was detached. I then also replaced him in a two-bedroom apartment on Massachussetts Avenue which I shared with Joe McCaffery, a Basic School classmate. Little Joe would be killed by a Japanese bullet in 1943 as he left his landing craft. Soon after I moved in, he was transferred to Quantico, and Dick Hayward* succeeded him at the Barracks and in the apartment. The Massachussetts Avenue where we lived was not the stately thoroughfare from Dupont Circle to the Washington Cathedral in northwest Washington, but Massachussetts Avenue, Southeast, a respectable but not smart address. Such a location would have been considered unacceptable for a married officer, who would have been expected to live in the northwest section, if he had not been assigned government quarters.

The only clothes we kept in our apartment were civilian except for the rarely worn evening or mess dress uniform and out-of-season service uniforms. We left for the Barracks in the morning and returned after duty hours properly turned out in civilian clothes. Service uniforms in season, as well as whites and blues, we kept in lockers in a small basement room at the Barracks where we changed upon arrival, and before departing in the afternoon. Officers in uniform were seldom seen in the nation's capital during the years between the two World Wars, before the building of the

*Brigadier General Richard W. Hayward, USMC (Ret).

Pentagon. Even enlisted personnel on duty at the War and Navy Departments wore civilian clothing. Of course, the uniform was worn at posts and stations within the District, but officers changed into civilian clothes before leaving them.

Those impressive titles, editor and publisher and assistant registrar, were misleading. As the latter I had little to do other than to sign an extraordinary amount of correspondence for the registrar, Lieutenant Colonel Shepherd. There were days when I signed my name steadily for more than an hour. I suppose that my title at the bottom of a note of encouragement and advice, which accompanied a lesson being returned to a student, was meant to convey to him that his effort had come to the attention of a school official of some importance. The Marine Corps Institute was operated almost entirely by selected NCOs who had more education than was usual among enlisted men, with the guidance of the International Correspondence Schools of Scranton, Pennsylvania. There were so many sergeants that some of them had to march in the ranks when the Institute Detachment was formed as a company.

The *Leatherneck*, a monthly magazine for marines, did not require much of my time because Technical Sergeant Frank H. Rentfrow had been producing the magazine for years with the help of a sergeant and three privates or privates first class. Rentfrow had tenure. It mattered little to him whether any of a succession of lieutenants, editor and publisher, had knowledge or experience in the field, so long as he was permitted a fairly free hand. During his off-duty hours at home (he was married), he wrote adventure stories for the pulps, not without success. A day or two after the current issue went to press he would begin to lay out the next. A slight man who seldom smiled but had a wry sense of humor, Rentfrow wrote much of the *Leatherneck*, which he edited and put together slumped patiently over his desk under an old green eye shade.

Printing and mailing were done by commercial contract. I handled the money through an account in a nearby bank. Enlisted correspondents at posts and stations throughout the Corps sent in what they considered to be newsworthy information every two or three months. In addition, one post or ship's detachment would be featured in each issue with a descriptive write-up. Having no office rent or staff salaries to pay (enlisted staff members received a modest stipend each month), the *Leatherneck* consistently stayed in the black. Surplus funds were kept within manageable proportions by spending more for illustrations.

The Barracks detachment was small and could parade only one company. For the most part, the members of the Marine Corps Institute Detachment sat at their desks correcting lessons on an upper floor. Occasionally they would participate in drills or, when needed, would form, together with the Barracks Detachment, the ceremonial battalion for a parade or a funeral escort at Arlington National Cemetery.

The United States Marine Band had been a national institution for more than a century. Its members were trained musicians enlisted specifically for the band with a special pay scale to attract talent. The band came under the commanding officer of the Barracks for administration, discipline, and routine ceremonial duties. It had been the president's band ever since Headquarters Marine Corps moved to Washington from Philadelphia in 1800. Because for many years it was the only musical resource available, the band had developed a special relationship with the White House that continued even after the larger services formed their bands in Washington more than a century later.

The Barracks had to provide funeral escorts and music for the burial in Arlington National Cemetery of deceased officers and men. Everyone at the Barracks and the surrounding neighborhood knew when a funeral detail of marines and bandsmen was about to leave for Arlington. Shortly before the busses were spotted at the main gate, the firing squad could be heard practicing their three volleys.

The duty was not unattractive. Arlington is beautiful. One marched with drawn sword in the procession from the Fort Myer chapel to the grave site along winding roads lined by tall trees which cast their shade over many monuments and gravestones. It came to mind that someday one's own remains might repose here. A timeless tranquillity pervades Arlington. Worrisome people, those of an impatient or turbulent turn of mind, may find peace there for an hour. High above the Potomac loom the thick columns of the mansion that was once the residence of Robert E. Lee.

The music we marched to was always the same, the Third Movement of Chopin's Sonata in B Flat Minor arranged for band, the stately expression of mourning for the heroic dead. Between the low-pitched chords, somber and inexorable, with which the movement begins and ends, there is that serene, wistful flight toward the everlasting. Now and then since that summer of 1935, a few bars of that music occasionally come to mind and I think fleetingly of Arlington.

Washington was a fascinating place in the middle 1930s. Although the Depression was severe, and young people begged in the streets, the activism of the New Deal in fighting it was exciting. The federal bureaucracy, referred to collectively as the "government clerks," was growing but was as yet only a fraction of what it has become. The War and Navy Departments were still in the temporary buildings lining the lower Mall on Constitution Avenue that they had occupied since the First World

War. The Department of State was supreme in the old State, War, and Navy Building which now, as the Executive Office Building, is an extension of the west wing of the White House.

Unlike today, officers on duty at the War and Navy Departments lived in the District and were a part of its life. The White House was more accessible than it has ever been since. It was open to tourists during the forenoon as now, but in the 1930s senior civil servants of the executive branch, senators and congressmen, and many Washington residents left cards at the White House early in the autumn. Officers of the armed services were required to do so. As the gates to the White House grounds on Pennsylvania Avenue were open during the day, one simply walked or drove to the portico. As one reached the topmost step and approached the door, it would be opened slightly by a black servant who offered a salver on which to drop one's cards. The consequence of this overture for persons of modest station such as lieutenants was an invitation to tea during the winter and perhaps another to a garden party on the south lawn later on in the spring.

One December afternoon, a lieutenant whom I shall call Lowell Huntingdon (that was not his name) and I presented ourselves at the east entrance dressed in our best dark civilian suits. We both had received engraved invitations which read, *Mrs. Roosevelt will be happy to receive,* followed by the handwritten name, date, and hour. Hunty was stationed at Quantico, where I had met him when I went there to call on Bobby Denig's parents. Colonel Denig was chief of staff at Quantico. That autumn Hunty was ordered to headquarters in Washington for temporary additional duty for several weeks. He possessed an automobile and frequently drove to Washington and returned to Quantico the same day. Sometimes, however, he spent the night in the spare bunk at our Massachussetts Avenue apartment. Hunty found Quantico dull after dark during the week. It was not very exciting to take a daughter of a field officer to the post movies. There was little scope for the basic urge, so, after his temporary duty at headquarters was finished, he continued to drive up to Washington two or three times a week after duty hours.

Having been only on temporary duty in Washington he was not required to leave cards at the White House. In fact he was not supposed to, but he arrived at the apartment one afternoon in October just as Dick Hayward and I were about to go to the White House to leave our cards. He gave us a lift there and on impulse left his own cards too. So there we were, entering the White House as guests of Mrs. Roosevelt. Dick had been invited a week earlier.

After leaving our coats and hats just inside, we moved casually along the lower corridor with other guests, pausing to look at the portraits. We had progressed a few steps beyond the cloakroom when Hunty became the victim of a grotesque, though hilarious, mischance. It was a consequence of having provided for a hoped-for requital later that evening, for he had a date. We had politely greeted a lieutenant colonel, who was on duty at headquarters, and his wife. As they walked on ahead of us Hunty paused to reach into a side pocket for a handkerchief. Finding none, as he afterward explained, he resorted to another displayed in his breast pocket. When he jerked it out in some exasperation at having forgotten the other, it launched in a graceful arc a rubber prophylactic device that fell on the floor about ten feet ahead of us. Fortunately there was no one between us and the lieutenant colonel.

Acting swiftly in this appalling crisis, Hunty leaped forward to put his foot over the neatly rolled white rubber sac, dropped the handkerchief he still held in his hand, and stooped casually to retrieve them both. I looked quickly about in all directions, apprehension and embarrassment struggling with an impulse to laugh, and drew close to Hunty.

"You got away with it. I'm certain no one saw it."

"Thank God," he muttered. "Never again."

"You mean to give up fornication?"

"No, you idiot. No more carrying these things loose in a pocket." That autumn Hunty had devoted many evenings in Washington to gathering data on the frailty of young women who worked in government offices. Convinced that a generous sampling would tend to validate his findings, he was ever on the lookout for fresh encounters.

We continued on to the staircase, adjusting our tendency to march to the leisurely pace of the straggling procession of guests. Ascending to the lobby we made our way to the east room, glancing at the gold piano as we proceeded toward the door to the green room at the south end. The guests lined up in a column of twos, closed up and halted, then began slowly to move again. Near the door to the green room a captain of cavalry, his gold aiguilletes worn on the right shoulder, formed the guests in single file, husbands preceding wives, and asked that we give our names distinctly to the next aide who would introduce us to Mrs. Roosevelt.

It was my first visit to the White House. Knowing that I should be able to enter it as a guest, I had not taken one of the morning public tours. We proceeded through the green room and into the blue room. I heard the Navy lieutenant announce, "Lieutenant Huntingdon," just before he inclined his head slightly toward me.

"Lieutenant Williams," I clearly enunciated.

"Lieutenant Williams."

"How do you do, Mrs. Roosevelt." Tall, not beautiful but womanly, singularly impressive, grand, she smiled in a friendly fashion, ever so gently propelling me past as we shook hands. Then it was on through the red room and into the state dining room for tea or coffee and cookies and a piece of cake. The receiving line finished, Mrs. Roosevelt joined the guests briefly without taking tea, trailed by the two aides. Making her way a few steps at a time, pausing occasionally to speak to someone, the First Lady reached the doorway to the main corridor through which she passed, attended by the aides, to enter the waiting elevator.

People began to leave. The two aides returned and accepted cups of tea from a lady whom they seemed to know who sat pouring at one end of the long table in the middle of the room. I was later to learn that she was Mrs. Helm, Mrs. Roosevelt's social secretary. Handsomely tailored in the undress blue uniforms of their services, the aides moved with good-natured assurance among the guests. I felt a hand on my arm. Hunty had the experienced party-goer's dread of being among the last to leave.

"Time we were off," he said. I nodded. We had been forty minutes in the executive mansion. The line of those invited for the second tea at five was forming. It was growing dark as we crossed Pennsylvania Avenue to stroll along the walk which traverses Lafayette Square diagonally, talking about the White House. We came to the statue of Andrew Jackson in the middle of the square, waving his fore and aft hat from his rearing horse to some distant throng. Our thoughts shifted to warfare in earlier times as we walked around this heroic figure to examine it in detail.

Continuing on, we reached the corner of the square opposite Decatur House. In that corner stands the bronze, cloaked figure of Baron von Steuben who inculcated George Washington's continentals with the rudiments of Prussian drill and maneuver. We were killing time, really. It was too soon after tea for a drink, but we were bound for the Army and Navy Club. Hunty had parked his car in the vacant lot next to the club on I Street.

We sauntered along what is seldom thought of as Connecticut Avenue—its short appendage south of Farragut Square. At the end of the block, at I Street, we paused for traffic beside the old red brick building that the club had occupied before the present building was erected across the street in 1912. I noticed that no pigeon squatted on the cap of the first American admiral's statue in the center of the little square, as one surely would have done earlier in the day. Suddenly the temptation to needle Hunty was irresistible.

"I suppose over the years the occupants of the White House have indulged in a normal amount of lovemaking in the bedrooms upstairs, but among all the millions of tourists who have trooped through the corridors and the thousands of invited guests who have danced in the East Room and dined at the other end since the time of President John Adams, you must be unique. Surely, no one else ever tossed a condom on the floor."

By this time we were mounting the steps to the front entrance of the club. He flushed, scowled, muttered angrily, "damn you, if you ever tell anyone. . . ." I threw back my head in uncontrollable laughter as memory played back the incident in the lower corridor. When my merriment subsided I clapped him on the back with one hand as I opened the outside door with the other. We entered to be greeted by Banks, the young doorman.

VIII

END OF A TOUR OF DUTY

On 5 April 1934, Major General John H. Russell, Jr., who had been U.S. high commissioner to Haiti for nine years during the 1920s, became the sixteenth commandant. He had but two years and eight months to serve because of the statutory age limit. In good weather, he frequently stepped outside the door of the sun porch entrance to the Commandant's House at sunset to stand evening colors. This was the occasion for an impromptu formality on the part of the officer of the day. "Keep an eye out for the MGC at evening colors," a newly joined officer would be advised when first taking over the duty. With the last note of "To the Color," before the bugler sounded "Carry On," the officer of the day who stood colors on the center walk would execute left face and salute. Being bareheaded and thus unable to return the salute, the Major General Commandant would nod perceptibly at about eighty yards.

General Russell liked things shipshape and grew dissatisfied with what he felt to be laxity in the performance of duty at the Barracks. Believing that smartness and discipline at 8th and I should be a model for the Corps, he ordered Colonel Emile P. Moses and Major Shepherd to Washington to be commanding officer and executive officer, respectively. Major Shepherd, who had been serving for four years in the Garde d'Haiti, arrived first. Pending Colonel Moses's return from the Far East, he was acting commanding officer for several weeks. (The previous CO had been retired.)

When Lem reported for duty, the Major General Commandant made it clear that corrective measures were in order to restore the post to exemplary status in smartness and discipline. General Russell had

Major General John H. Russell, 16th commandant, 1934–1936. Courtesy U.S. Marine Corps.

selected the right officer for his purpose. With such a mandate Major Shepherd eagerly took over command of the Barracks. The slack routine changed almost overnight, although it took several weeks of continuing effort by all hands to achieve the commandant's goal.

As always in a renewal of the pursuit of excellence, the emphasis was on the fundamentals: smartness in bearing and comportment of the individual marine, and precise execution of close order drill. These are the basis for perfecting the ceremonial performance of platoon, company, and battalion. Formal guard mount daily at 0800 preceded an inspection and practice parade of the entire command. On Saturday mornings, which were reserved for commanding officer's inspection in blues, Major Shepherd looked searchingly at each officer and man for imperfections in uniform, arms, and equipment.

The officers and men of the Barracks Detachment, the Marine Corps Institute, and the U.S. Marine Band responded well to the new routine. As they say in the Navy, "a taut ship is a happy ship." Major Shepherd also required all post buglers to march behind the band and participate in the parts of the marches written for the trumpet. This modest beginning of the splendid present-day Drum and Bugle Corps led to a difficult assignment for Major Shepherd. Brigadier General Douglas C. Macdougald, the assistant commandant who occupied the quarters next to the commandant's garden, directed Shepherd to write a manual for the drum and bugle as well as the fife. Unendowed with musical talent, Lem was dismayed at first, but with the help of the leader of the band, considerable research, and recollections of the manner in which tenor drummers of British regimental bands in Shanghai used to twirl their sticks, he produced the *Manual for Drummers, Trumpeters and Fifers, U.S. Marine Corps, 1935.*

When Colonel Moses reported for duty, the commandant must have mentioned his dissatisfaction with the previous commanding officer and described with approval Lem's corrective action. The new commanding officer gladly took over direction of the new routine which Lem continued to implement as executive officer. The daily practice parades were soon discontinued as details were worked out for a weekly parade in blues to which the public would be invited. Colonel Moses decided to hold it each Monday afternoon during the warmer months, that being Mrs. Russell's day at home. Later, Friday became parade day.

The U.S. Marine Band has been part of the Barracks complement since the post was established in 1801. The bill that President John Adams signed into law in 1798 creating the Marine Corps provided for thirty-two drummers and fifers but not a band. Band instruments and persons who could play them were scarce in America at the turn of the nineteenth century, but Lieutenant Colonel Commandant Burrows, determined to have a proper band, set about purchasing instruments and obtaining musicians. Congress having appropriated no funds for such an endeavor, Burrows demanded a small monthly contribution from each officer to defray the expense. On Independence Day 1800, the United States Marine Band gave its first public concert, in Philadelphia. Then came the move, with Headquarters Marine Corps, to the new City of Washington and the first public concert there in August. On New Years Day 1801, the band first played at the White House for a reception given by President and Mrs. Adams. A few weeks later, on 4 March, it participated in the inauguration of Thomas Jefferson. The last two occasions established precedents.

President Jefferson suggested to the commandant that he obtain Italian musicians. Burrows therefore directed the marine officer on board the frigate *Chesapeake*, which sailed for the Mediterranean in 1803, to recruit some. When the *Chesapeake* returned in 1805 with sixteen musicians and their families, there was consternation at the Barracks. Burrows, who was

John Philip Sousa, a portrait by Capolina of the leader of the band from 1880 to 1892. Courtesy U.S. Marine Corps.

The U. S. Marine Band, Captain Branson Taylor, leader, with the Capitol of the United States in the background (about 1930). Courtesy U.S. Marine Corps Museum.

no longer commandant, had neglected to inform his successor, Franklin Wharton, of the plan to enlist Italians. Somehow the matter was resolved and the Italians were taken into the band. Their musical skills probably improved its performance. The band has always been available to the President. In 1863 Abraham Lincoln took the band with him to Gettysburg where he spoke a few words in dedication of the battlefield after two hours of oratory by Edward Everett.

The name and fame of John Philip Sousa live on in memory and stirring sound as the band he led continues to play his famous marches. He was leader from 1880 to 1892. His father, a trombonist in the band, arranged for him to enlist as an apprentice at the age of thirteen. In 1875 Sousa left the band to conduct musical comedies and operettas, but the commandant later brought him back as leader. His first appearance as such, after a thorough reorganization of the band, was at the New Year's Day reception of President Hayes on 1 January 1881. After having served as leader under five Presidents, Sousa left again to form his own band.

Since Sousa's time, the U.S. Marine Band has been essentially a concert band but also one that can parade a superb marching band of 100 down Pennsylvania Avenue on great national occasions and cause the hearts of spectators to swell when it crashes into "The Stars and Stripes Forever." For more than 175 years, it has played at all occasions of state and provided music for dinners and receptions at the White House.

When I reported for duty at the Barracks in 1935, Captain Taylor Branson, who had enlisted in the band in 1898, was leader. Until Major Shepherd arrived in 1934, the band had seldom appeared on the parade ground with troops since before the First World War.

Now, performing in the humbler role of post band, it rather dwarfed the improvised ceremonial battalion augmented by a platoon from the Navy Yard barracks. Soon after I reported for duty, I became parade adjutant. Summer parade uniform was white cap, blue blouse, white trousers and gloves. About two minutes before the hour, I emerged from the officers' dressing room in the basement near the flagpole to proceed along the arcade toward the Commandant's House. At the corner I turned left to continue past the right flank of the band and along the iron fence. As I reached the little gate, I saluted the Major General Commandant who, with Mrs. Russell and a few guests, was standing in the garden to watch the ceremony. I then turned left again to continue along officers' row to the center walk. There I made a third left, proceeded a few steps toward the flagpole, and halted. As the time orderly prepared to strike two bells, I drew my sword. After the second stroke, I sang out, "Sound adjutant's call."

The U. S. Marine Band at the Blue and Grey Reunion at Gettysburg in July 1938 during the 75th anniversary year of the dedication of Gettysburg. Courtesy U.S. Marine Corps Museum.

It was still the day of the eight-man squad formed in two ranks and the old "squads right" drill. The ceremony of parade (as distinguished from a street parade) can be a stirring experience for the participants as well as for the spectators. As a spectacle it is all straight lines and right angles made by uniformed, armed men who stand erect and motionless except when, at the word of command, they execute precise movements with their weapons or march in cadence to the sound of drums and martial music. As an exercise for those participating, it is an intense effort, individual and collective, to achieve perfection of performance. It means utter immobility save for breathing and closing and opening the eyelids while standing at attention or at parade rest; all rifles carried on the shoulder at the same angle and held perpendicular at present arms; the simultaneous crash of many palms smacking rifle stocks and slings in certain movements of the manual of arms; the grounding together of many rifle butts when coming to order arms; and the flashing sweep in unison of officers' swords when saluting the parade commander at officers center.

The preoccupation of the military with ceremonial amuses, even irritates, people who fail to understand that the observable behaviour of a command reflects the level of discipline, morale, and esprit de corps within. Strict observance of military courtesy and conformity in doing

The band serenades the commandant on New Year's Day, 1927. General Lejeune stands beside Captain William H. Santleman in the center. Second leader Taylor Branson, who would become leader when Santleman retired on 1 May of that year, stands in the foreground to the right front of the commandant.

everything in the line of duty in the manner prescribed, from the rendering of the salute to the review and inspection of a division, mold and nurture pride and self-confidence.

The summer of 1935 passed. Greens (winter service) became the uniform of the day. Autumn became winter and the parade season was long past. The calendar got to Christmas and the year of our Lord one thousand nine hundred and thirty-five ran out its days. On 1 January 1936 the officers of the Barracks and their ladies (as officers' wives were usually referred to then) were invited to the Commandant's House for the traditional New Year's Day serenade. Invitations nowadays are for a later hour than they were then. The gathering has also become much larger in recent years, with slowly circulating guests filling all the rooms on the second and third floors of the wonderful old house as well as the stairs and the reception rooms, dining room, and solarium downstairs. In 1936 the commandant and Mrs. Russell invited only a few friends, both military and civilian.

A few minutes before noon, the musicians of the band entered the garden from the parade ground gate to form on the lawn near the steps to the sun porch entrance. At noon, Captain Branson, in the magnificence of the leader's special full dress uniform of an older time and wearing a sword, raised his baton to begin the first of two or three selections. With the approach of the band, General Russell had gone out on the sun porch stoop.

After the first group, the leader faced about and wished the commandant a Happy New Year from the members of the band. General Russell expressed his appreciation to the band, praised them for their outstanding work during the previous year, and invited them to come in for eggnog after the serenade. Then the "Stars and Stripes for Ever," followed by the "Marine Corps Hymn," and up the steps and into the house the musicians came, leaving their instruments on the sun porch. After being received by General and Mrs. Russell, they passed on into the dining room for eggnog and something to eat as the invited guests were leaving.

My tour of duty at the Barracks came to an unexpected end in February 1936. I was to have remained there a year before being ordered to the Infantry School at Fort Benning, Georgia. It was desirable to be a graduate of that Army school as the Quantico Schools had not yet attained the stature they would soon have. Most first lieutenants and captains attended the Junior Course at Quantico; only four marine officers were sent to the Infantry School each year.

Paul Sherman had returned from Shanghai and was on duty at the Navy Yard barracks, hoping to go to law school. He occupied public quarters, an upper-floor apartment in the Latrobe Gate complex meant for a married officer. One day in January, he and Dick Hayward and I and another "China hand" dined together and later stopped in at the Troika, a nightclub on Connecticut Avenue near the Mayflower Hotel. Vodka was an uncommon drink in America then, but we had learned to drink it in Shanghai, cold and straight in a shot glass, in the Russian manner.

Three couples took a table adjacent to ours. Gathering from their conversation that they were Army, we introduced ourselves. They proved to be lieutenants, a few years out of West Point, accompanied by their wives. We put the tables together, a mistake as we found out at the one o'clock closing hour after a pleasant evening of drinking and dancing. After the Army couples had paid their check and left, we were presented with a staggering one. No four men could drink that much vodka and walk, and we knew our friends had paid their share.

Dick and I protested vigorously, too vigorously, and demanded to see the manager. It was of no use. Our companions, who were becoming uneasy, went downstairs to the street. There had not been enough cash among the four of us. There were no credit cards in those days so Dick began to write a check. Standing a few feet behind him I watched with growing apprehension as a man in blue walked to his side and waited for him to finish writing. Police! When Dick had signed the check the policeman put a hand on his shoulder. At the same time I felt a hand on one of mine. We went quietly and passed about two hours in jail in separate cells. Eventually, the officer of the day at the Barracks, Captain Ridgely, was notified of our plight and persuaded the police to release us.

We then repaired to Paul Sherman's quarters at the Navy Yard to review the evening. The night was far gone when we found our beds. Either we forgot to set the alarm or we slept through it. When we awoke it was long past 0800. We entered the main gate about 1100, too late for me to relieve Captain Ridgely as officer of the day, an unforgivable dereliction of duty.

As we were getting into uniform in the basement dressing room, shining our leather with special care, we received word to report to the executive officer. When we entered his office, he was talking to Captain Ridgely. Lieutenant Colonel Shepherd told us that the commanding officer wished to see us and immediately led the way to the latter's office. Ridgely, of course, had made an entry in the guard book concerning our difficulty with the police.

Dick and I stood stiffly at attention before Colonel Clarke's desk as he listened to Captain Ridgely's recital of unusual nocturnal events. When asked if the substance of his account was correct, we answered, "yes, Sir." When asked whether either of us had anything to say in extenuation we replied, "no, Sir."

"That is all then, gentlemen, for the moment." We about faced and marched out. The executive officer had a word for us. "Don't go to duty," he advised. "Stay in the dressing room until I send for you."

After twenty minutes, we were told to report to the executive officer. "Well, gentlemen," Lieutenant Colonel Shepherd said gravely, "I'm afraid I have to ask for your swords. Report back to me here at 1400. Uniform: undress blues with swords. Colonel Clarke had to go to headquarters. He asked me to inform you both that he has awarded you ten days arrest in quarters."

We had something to eat in the general mess, changed into blues and put on our swords. Brother officers we chanced to encounter nodded but did not speak. We reported back to the executive officer as directed. He gave us each a typed order signed by Colonel Clarke which we read.

"Any questions?" asked Colonel Shepherd. We had none. "You will note," he said, "that the period of arrest begins upon receipt of the arrest orders. You will therefore leave your quarters ten days from today in time to change into the uniform of the day and report to me here at 1400 to receive back your swords. And now, gentlemen, your swords." We removed them from the sword slings on our Sam Browne belts and handed them to him.

"Very well," he said. "Change into civilian clothes and go to your quarters."*

It was a long ten days. We learned more about cooking. During the hour allowed us each morning and afternoon for exercise and to buy groceries we walked at a fast pace. Friends told us that they heard the Major General Commandant was furious when informed of our misconduct and spoke of a general court-martial.

Colonel Clarke's award of ten days arrest may have forestalled the taking of more serious disciplinary action. He could have recommended a general court-martial, but apparently he considered that to be excessive. Instead he quickly awarded us arrest to present General Russell with an accomplished fact should the latter urge him to recommend a general court-martial. It was possible that the colonel had concluded that our failure to report for duty on time was the real offense. Despite having been jailed for two hours no civil charges were preferred. We had not been in uniform. There was no mention of the incident at the Troika in the newspapers, and there had been reason to protest the bill which we had paid.

General Russell refused, however, to have either of us at the Barracks any longer. When we reported to Colonel Shepherd at the end of ten days to repossess our swords he handed each of us permanent change of station orders. Dick Hayward went to the Recruit Depot at Parris Island. I was to proceed to Edgewood Arsenal, Maryland, to attend a three-month course about to begin at the Army's Chemical Warfare School.

Before leaving, I went to headquarters to see the director of personnel, Colonel John Marston, whom I knew, to ask about my projected assignment to the Infantry School in September.

"Benning?" he asked in surprise. "Oh, no. I've already replaced you on the list." He shook his head. "It's out of my hands."

---

*The commanding officer of a post or regiment could award an officer under his command up to ten days arrest in quarters, relieved of all duty, for an offense he did not consider serious enough for him to recommend general court-martial, which only a general officer could award. This punishment was not unusual until after the selection system of promotion became law in 1934. After two or three years under the new system, commanding officers realized that to punish an officer with arrest was apt to end his career when next he was considered for promotion. As a consequence this punishment became extremely rare.

IX

REDEMPTION

Edgewood Arsenal, the Chemical Warfare Center of the Army, was a military reservation near Chesapeake Bay between Baltimore and Havre de Grace. Civil service scientists were secretly developing nerve gases and experimenting with protective uniform clothing to neutralize the burning effect of mustard gas on the skin, so dreaded during the First World War.

The purpose of the Chemical Warfare School was less to train officers for the Chemical Warfare Service than it was to qualify officers of the combat branches to serve as chemical warfare staff officers at brigade and division levels. The only chemical warfare company of the Army, fully motorized and armed with 4.2-inch chemical mortars, conducted field tests and school demonstrations.

I completed the course in May, but Headquarters Marine Corps decided to keep me there longer, attached to the chemical company, to become familiar with the 4.2-inch mortar and to learn more about protective clothing. In August there was a field test of the latter for which I had volunteered to spend what promised to be an uncomfortably dull week.

There were eight of us, an old-drill infantry squad of officers, who lived under canvas in field conditions reasonably simulating a combat situation. For six days it was necessary to wear protective clothing without removing it. We were not exposed to mustard gas, as the clothing had already been successfully tested for its neutralizing effect. Rather, this field test was intended to determine whether troops could operate under war conditions for an appreciable period while wearing such clothing.

For two hours each morning and again each afternoon, we performed tasks which an infantry squad might have to do while exposed to mustard gas—marching, digging foxholes, firing rifles, and so on. It was hot work under the August sun of Maryland because we also wore gas masks and gloves which left no skin exposed. One's face sweated profusely into the mask, forming a pool under the chin which splashed around the cheeks and nostrils. Medical officers regularly checked our hearts and blood pressure. Except during these periods, we removed masks, gloves, and helmets, but nothing else. Although we smelled like goats toward the end of the week, we did have time for cards and reading. Having read a pre-publication review of a book in the *New York Times*, I had sent for a copy which arrived just in time. On the last day I finished reading that lengthy but fascinating book, *Gone with the Wind*.

In October, orders arrived for me to proceed to Quantico and report to the commanding general, 1st Marine Brigade, Fleet Marine Force. The prospect of serving in the FMF appealed to me, but I was not enthusiastic about what ten years later would be called my military occupational specialty, chemical warfare. A small chemical company of one platoon was to be activated in March 1937, after the brigade returned from Fleet Landing Exercise Number Three on the West Coast. I was to serve as both company commander and brigade chemical officer. Although I preferred the infantry, the prospect of escaping the coldest months and going through the canal again to learn the techniques of landing operations in California was attractive.

When I reported for duty, the 1st Marine Brigade, Fleet Marine Force, was not quite three years old, an embryo force of combined arms organized around an infantry core. The 5th Marines consisted of two small battalions at peacetime strength. There were only 1,500 enlisted men in the entire brigade, half the strength of an infantry regiment of the Second World War. Marine Aircraft One, a composite group composed of squadrons of different types (fighting, bombers, observation, utility), provided air support. Major General Charles H. Lyman commanded the post, Brigadier General James G. Meade the brigade, and Brigadier General Thomas Holcomb the schools.

Visions of the Panama Canal and sandy California beaches soon faded. In war and peace, combat formations invariably designate a small administrative remnant called the rear echelon which misses all the fun. One officer on the brigade staff had to remain at Quantico. The chief of staff decided that it should be the brigade chemical officer, the most recently joined and easiest to spare, since the problems of chemical warfare were not to be addressed to any extent in the exercise.

So a bleak winter lay ahead, but November 1936 was an exciting month. Tuesday, the third, was election day, and it brought a landslide victory for President Roosevelt. When he returned to Washington after a few days at Hyde Park, 200,000 people jammed Union Station Plaza to greet him. It was remarked in the press that their mood was more like that of a crowd welcoming home a popular sports figure than a President.

On Saturday 7 November, at the Navy-Notre Dame football game in Baltimore, an expectant hush descended on the crowd of 57,000 as Navy left halfback Bill Ingram awaited the snap from center in the third quarter. He drop-kicked the ball between the goal posts for the only score of the game.

On Sunday 8 November, the Washington papers reported that 50,000 rebels under General Franco were storming the gates of Madrid, and that in England, the uncrowned but reigning King Edward VIII continued to discard tradition. Instead of using the royal "we, us, and our" in an address to the Lords and Commons proroguing Parliament the previous week, he had said "I, me, and my." Ominously the London papers had begun to break silence on the King's friend, Mrs. Simpson, whose petition for divorce would soon be granted and whose movements the U.S. press had been reporting for some weeks.

On Monday 9 November, two of the King's subjects, Noel Coward and Gertrude Lawrence, opened at the National Theater in "Tonight at Eight-Thirty," nine hilarious one-act plays by Coward, presented in groups of three on Monday, Wednesday, and Friday "first nights." A note on one of the society pages under a Quantico dateline informed readers that Brigadier General and Mrs. Thomas Holcomb would entertain sixty guests at dinner at the officers' club on Tuesday 10 November, the 161st birthday anniversary of the Corps.

During the first ten days of November 1936, ships' detachments, marine barracks, and expeditionary units worldwide were expecting an "All-Nav" message from the Secretary of the Navy. This was to announce whom the President had selected to replace General Russell as Major General Commandant when he retired on 1 December at the statutory age. The name of the new Chief of Naval Operations would also be announced, but that was almost a certainty whereas there was no certainty about the next commandant.

Marine officers were about equally divided in their support for Major General Louis McCarty Little, assistant to the commandant (the successor apparent), and Major General Lyman. Word went about that Louis Little, a man of great charm, and Mrs. Little, the former Elsie Cobb Wilson, had dined with the President and Mrs. Roosevelt. This was not thought to be a mark of favor by many, however. The President would never tip his hand in so obvious a way. Nor, having been assistant secretary for almost eight years, would the President have been much influenced by any recommendation of his Secretary of the Navy, Claude

More than half of the general officers of the Marine Corps of 1935 appear in this photograph in evening dress uniform. They watch Major General Commandant John H. Russell prepare to cut the cake at the Marine Corps birthday ball at Quantico in 1935. Major General Louis McCarty Little is second from the left. Major General Charles H. Lyman is to the commandant's left. Brigadier General Thomas Holcomb, on the far right, would be appointed Major General Commandant to succeed Russell just one year later. Courtesy U.S. Marine Corps.

Swanson, who paid little attention to the Marine Corps. After the event it was said that the President, aware of the strong feeling within the Corps, had asked to see the service records of several brigadier generals.

On the morning of 10 November, General and Mrs. Holcomb motored to Washington. Probably the general was told of his selection, but it was a well-kept secret until the public announcement that afternoon. On their way back to Quantico the Holcombs heard over the radio that Admiral William D. Leahy would become Chief of Naval Operations and Brigadier General Thomas Holcomb, Commandant of the Marine Corps.

That evening the dining room of the officers club was reserved for dinner parties given by ranking officers and their wives. All the guests became general-watchers. The gaiety of the Holcomb party was contagious. I had only seen General Holcomb once before. His appearance could not be described as distinguished, but certainly as solid and reassuring. He was of medium height, balding, stockily built, and wore glasses. One sensed that he possessed deep reservoirs of common sense, and a

The Major General Commandant, Thomas Holcomb, on the rifle range at Camp Perry, Ohio, in 1937 during the national matches. Note the distinguished marksman medal that he wears beneath his service ribbons. As a young officer, General Holcomb had several times been a member of the Marine Corps team that participated annually in those matches. Courtesy U.S. Marine Corps.

capacity to see things through after making careful decisions. Not really being acquainted with any of the generals, it seemed to me that the President had made a good choice. At the time, however, this surprising announcement on the Marine Corps birthday had no apparent bearing on my immediate future.

One bright spot remained in November before a dull winter. Bobby Denig and Mary Drake were to be married in Richmond. He had returned from China during the summer and had spent a weekend with me at Edgewood Arsenal. Since September he had been a student at the Army Tank School at Fort Benning. Mary had returned with her mother after her father's death in Hong Kong. The wedding was on Thanksgiving weekend and great fun. It began with a bachelor dinner at the Commonwealth Club with champagne glasses thrown into the fireplace after a toast to the bride. Luncheon and afternoon parties followed the next day. It was an evening wedding with four ushers and myself as best man giving moral support to the groom, all in the gold-braided finery of the evening dress uniform. This was but a weekend interlude, however, to the daily staff talk at Quantico that did not concern me about embarkation in January for the fleet landing exercise and the big parade at the San Diego Base. Both brigades of the FMF were to be formed for a review and inspection during which both marine aircraft groups would do a flyover.

On the first day of December 1936, Thomas Holcomb took office as the seventeenth Commandant of the Marine Corps. On 14 December telephonic orders instructed me to proceed to Headquarters Marine Corps for one day's temporary duty and to report to the Major General Commandant at 1100 the following morning.

When I entered the aides' office just before the appointed hour, a smiling young man a little older than I rose from behind a desk to greet me, introducing himself as Paul Drake. After indicating where I could hang my coat and hat, he peered discreetly over the top of the louvered swinging door before pushing on through. Reappearing in the doorway he motioned for me to enter. As I marched past him to halt at attention in front of the desk, Captain Drake spoke my name and withdrew. The quiet figure behind the desk looked up briefly, scarcely moving his head and gestured toward a chair to his right.

"Have a chair, Williams," said the Major General Commandant, and resumed reading some report. Presently he straightened up and turned slightly in his chair to regard me in silence, registering neither approval nor disapproval.

"Well," he said finally, "do you believe you now have under control what some people who know you regard as a slight tendency to drink a little too much now and then?"

"Yes, Sir. I believe so."

"Would you like to be one of my aides?"

"Yes, Sir."

"Very well. I'm supposed to have three. You may have noticed a vacant desk out there. Oh, yes. You don't expect to marry in the near future, do you? Because you will also be appointed an aide at the White House."

"No, Sir."

"Well, that's settled then," he remarked, with the mild satisfaction a busy man might allow himself after having disposed of another small but bothersome problem.

"Drake," he called out, as he pressed a buzzer. Captain Drake returned as I rose with the commandant who told him, "tell the Detail Office to issue permanent change of station orders for your new colleague. Williams is going to join us." He offered his hand and pressed mine warmly. Trying to control a surging elation, I returned to the aides' office to be introduced to the senior aide who had been occupied with the telephone when I arrived.

"You'll get proceed orders, probably tomorrow. That will give you four days to clear out of Quantico and find a place to live here in Washington. You might try the Baronet. Right up the street." We were standing near the large second-story windows, and he gestured toward 18th Street below. "Just a nice walk. It's next to the corner on H Street where H runs into Pennsylvania Avenue, across the street from the Powhatan Hotel. Nice place. Not large. About eight partly furnished bachelor apartments. Living room, bedroom, bath, entrance hall, daily maid service, but no kitchen."

"Thanks," I said, as I got into my overcoat. "I've never been an aide. I seem to be starting at the top."

"Don't worry about it. You'll have to learn your way around the place, of course. When you report for duty I'll take you on a tour of all the offices. All the powers that be will have a look at you and you'll be able to identify most of them the next time you see them. It's a little difficult until you know all the officers by sight, with everyone in civilian clothes.

"Clyde, here, is a White House aide. He can cue you in on that part of it, but that won't be until sometime next year. The naval aide to the President must have a look at you first."

Still dazed by this sudden smile of fortune, I walked north on 18th Street past Constitution Hall, past the Octagon House where President Madison and the charming Dolley lived while the White House was undergoing repair. The world seemed a wonderful planet and a commission in the Marine Corps a matchless possession.

Crossing Pennsylvania Avenue, I passed the entrance to the Powhatan (or Roger Smith) Hotel to cross H Street and find the Baronet at number 1737. There was a vacancy. Shown a handsome old apartment with high ceilings and floors which my Peking rugs would fit nicely, I signed a year's lease at seventy-five dollars a month, wrote a check for a month's rent, and walked three blocks to the Army and Navy Club for a drink and a light lunch in the bar before returning to Union Station to take a train back to Quantico.

X

AIDE TO THE
MAJOR GENERAL COMMANDANT

The French noun *aide* means one who assists another. Initially *aide de camp* signified an officer attached to the person, as distinguished from the staff, of a general officer commanding in the field. The general might refer to his aides de camp, often relatively young officers of field or company grade, as his official family. The relationship between the commander and his aides was warm but formal, comparable to that between sons and a distinguished and still active father. The aides took their meals at the general's table. One or two invariably accompanied him wherever he went, on social as well as military occasions.

On active service the commander of an army might have had six or eight aides. Before the day of the telephone and the radio these young officers were the means whereby the general transmitted his orders to subordinate commanders in camp or bivouac, on the march, and during deployment and battle. They were also extensions of his eyes and ears. Upon cantering back from a mission to a corps or a division, an aide was often required to give the commander his impressions of its state of morale and discipline.

In garrison during peacetime fewer aides were needed. Most of them returned to their regiments. With the advent of the radio and mechanization, and the consequent dispersion of forces in contrast to their former close deployment in the day of the horse and the musket, the role of the aide was modified. His duties in the field on active service came to resemble more closely those he performed in garrison in peacetime.

In 1936 general officers commanding rated aides, as they do today. The French noun had become an English word but the modifying phrase

The old "Tempo," now gone, on the Mall facing Constitution Avenue between 17th and 19th Streets. Shown is the main entrance at 18th Street. From 1919 until the Second World War, Headquarters Marine Corps occupied offices on the second floor to the left. Courtesy U.S. Marine Corps.

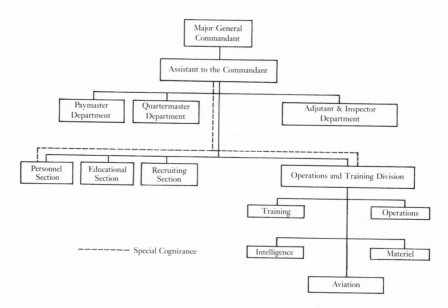

Headquarters U.S. Marine Corps as reorganized by General Lejeune in 1920. (Headquarters Memorandum 1 December 1920).

was obsolescent. Old regulations might refer to aides de camp, but they were called aides. These young officers, who reported to no one but their general, formed a protective zone around him. Officers and visitors who wished to see the general had first to pass through the aides' office, which adjoined his. The chief of staff or a second in command might have his office on the other side of the commander, whose office he might enter unannounced. Perhaps one or two other senior officers had ready access and could walk through the aides' office with only a questioning glance to make certain that the general was alone, but this privilege was enjoyed by no one else.

On the December morning of 1936 that I reported for duty, I was immediately thrust into the unfamiliar stream of headquarters activity. First there was an informal talk with General Holcomb so that he could tell me something of what he expected of me. There were two guiding principles. One was discretion. Occasions would arise when I might hear things discussed that obviously ought not to be repeated. It was probably the best course to make it a rule not to mention at all, anywhere, what went on at headquarters during the day. Then there was the matter of accurateness when he was seeking information. He said he would put questions to me or the other aides sometimes.

"Don't give me an unqualified answer unless you are certain. If you don't know the answer, or aren't certain, say so at once and go and find out. Understood?"

"Yes, General Holcomb."

"All right. Go to it. Glad to have you on board. We must see to it that you meet Mrs. Holcomb soon. Drake is going to take you on the grand tour this morning, I believe."

In December 1936, headquarters consisted of fifty-three officers and ninety-four enlisted personnel. Its organization was much as it was in 1920 when General Lejeune, soon after taking office as commandant, had added a division of operations and training to the existing structure of three staff departments and several separate sections. The director of the division of operations and training and those of the separate sections were subject to transfer and replacement by the new commandant. Similarly the assistant to the commandant, who had special cognizance over them.

The heads of the staff departments, on the other hand, the paymaster, the quartermaster, and the adjutant and inspector—all brigadier generals—were fixtures. Their duties and prerogatives were to a degree defined by law. Once in office they could not be transferred and replaced. Of long standing, administrative and supportive in nature, the staff departments were vital to the operation and well-being of the Corps. They participated little, however, in decisions as to what functions the Corps should have and for what contingencies it should be prepared. That was the province of the commandant, his assistant, and the director of the division of operations and training.

During the remainder of the morning Drake led me from office to office, from those of the general officers to the mail room, the communications center manned by a warrant officer and NCO messengers. There were to be only two significant changes in headquarters personnel because of a new commandant taking office. General Little, who had been a major general when Holcomb was only a brigadier general, was in a false position as assistant to the commandant, but apparently this could wait until the usual end-of-tour transfers that took place throughout the Corps during June and July. The two seemed to have found a way to accept the situation for a few months, but General Holcomb wanted Holland M. Smith to be his director of operations and training. Colonel Smith was chief of staff of the Department of the Pacific in San Francisco. There was no difficulty about ordering him to Washington, but another officer of the same name, Colonel Julian M. Smith, had become director the previous July and would normally remain so until the summer of 1938. The matter was happily resolved by ordering the director of personnel, Colonel John Marston, to his new post as commanding officer of the Embassy Guard in Peking several months ahead of his scheduled transfer date and moving Julian Smith over to personnel.

We aides were junior in rank to almost all other officers serving at headquarters, not that we were so youthful, however. The senior aide had served in France in 1918. At twenty-nine, I was the only lieutenant on the headquarters muster roll. As aides we did not contribute directly to the task of running the Marine Corps or solving the problems which daily confronted the commandant. We worked on no staff studies, served on no boards, did not assist in the formulation of policy. Yet, because of our proximity to General Holcomb, we sensed a certain respect (perhaps grudging in a few cases), as we walked among and talked to our seniors who carried the work load.

General Holcomb arrived at 0830, so I left the Baronet at 0800 for the fifteen-minute walk down 18th Street. The day at the aides' office began with one of us standing by the telephone, ready to greet the commandant when he came in, while the others went to the cafeteria for coffee. Our large desks, seldom cluttered with paperwork, formed a flat-topped mass in the center of the room. Paul Drake's desk and mine were front to front, so that we faced each other when seated. The senior aide's desk abutted them. Looking beyond Drake, I could see the swinging louvered door, rather like a gate, to the commandant's office. Glancing obliquely left I could see the senior aide at his desk and behind him the outer wall of the

Brown Field, Marine Barracks, Quantico, Virginia, 6 Sept. 1940. Major General
Commandant Thomas Holcomb (left) is talking to Lieutenant Colonel Field
Harris (center), commanding officer of what had been Aircraft One, redesignated
1st Marine Aircraft Group in May 1939. On the right is Brigadier General
Holland M. Smith, commanding the 1st Marine Brigade, Fleet Marine Force.
Courtesy U.S. Marine Corps.

building which was largely windowpane. I had to shift my gaze ninety
degrees to the right, however, to see anyone entering from the corridor. A
clerk/typist, a young marine who attended night school, sat at a small desk
in one corner reading law during his spare moments.

There were two telephones which we could push back and forth to
each other while seated. One was our own. Like all new aides, during the
first few days I heard the commandant's telephone ring with a sinking

feeling because the old hands, pushing it toward me if necessary, would wait for me to take the call. The first few times I picked up the receiver and said in a friendly voice, "Commandant's office, Lieutenant Williams speaking," I would shortly have to put my hand over the mouthpiece to ask for guidance. Many calls from outside the Navy Department had to be redirected to the proper staff section without bothering the general. The senior aide was the commandant's liaison with the U.S. Marine Band. A bachelor, he was also a White House aide. Drake, who was married, attended to matters concerning the Commandant's House.

The commandant's office would seem unimpressive in its spartan plainness compared with those of the secretaries and officers who head the services today. General Holcomb had no luncheon mess. Unless the weather was bad, he and H.M. Smith and perhaps a department head or later the secretary to the commandant, would walk over to the new building of the Department of the Interior. It was a little to the north of Constitution Avenue and had a more attractive cafeteria.

There was no separate dining room for officers in the Navy building, or even a space reserved for them in the large cafeteria. Few left the building for lunch. The Army and Navy Club was too far away unless one had the afternoon off, and except on those days it was not customary to go anywhere where cocktails were served. Some senior officers might have a tray brought to their desks, but not the Chief of Naval Operations. It was not unusual to be standing in line and see Admiral Leahy patiently sliding his tray along the counter. Most officers skimped on the noon meal. It was good for the pocketbook as well as the waistline.

A few days after I reported for duty, the commandant had an unexpected visitor. It may have been the first time that I was "holding the fort" alone. About mid-morning while the others were taking a coffee break in the cafeteria, I was startled by the entrance of a tall, gray-haired man. I stood up, astonished to meet the oncoming gaze of General Holcomb's predecessor in office who had summarily terminated my tour of duty at the Barracks earlier in the year. "Is the commandant alone?" he asked. "I just wish to see him for a moment to say good-bye."

"I believe he is, general. Just a moment." As I moved quickly past him to enter the commandant's office, I recalled having read that General and Mrs. Russell planned to live in retirement on the West Coast. He was probably making the rounds in the department, saying farewell to old friends.

"General Russell is here to see you, General Holcomb." The commandant looked up, put down one of four pipes he smoked in rotation, and said, "Well, show him in." As he rose to move around his desk in polite greeting I held the door open. General Russell seemed to pause in the doorway but without really stopping he regarded me gravely for a moment. With a suggestion of a smile he said in a barely audible aside, "Good luck in your new assignment."

The recently retired Major General Commandant and the new incumbent represented the leaders of two categories into which all field and general officers of the Corps could be divided, those who had fought in France and those who had not. Although fewer in number, those of the first category could be identified by the bronze battle stars on their rainbow-colored victory medal ribbons and by the fourragère on their left shoulders.

Many of the officers who had not fought in France, of course, had had active service experience elsewhere. They also wore campaign ribbons and sometimes others representing decorations, even that of the Medal of Honor, but these had been earned while on expeditionary duty. These officers had missed the greatest of wars up to that time. The two groups could not be described as factions, and their rivalry, although perhaps tinged with some envy on the part of those who had not had a chance to fight the Germans, was unspoken. Each group, however, took a little satisfaction in having one of its own living-in the Commandant's House.

General Russell had not served in France and in 1919 had been president of the selection board that had shown no favor to the young temporary and reserve officers of the 4th Brigade who had applied for permanent commissions. The appointments of General Russell and his predecessor General Fuller (Major General Commandant 1930–1934) had interrupted the postwar tendency to appoint an officer to head the Corps from among those who had fought in France. This change was partly because there had been no officers of sufficient seniority to be considered after General Neville (Major General Commandant 1929–1930). General Russell had wanted his assistant, Louis McCarty Little, to succeed him.

Thomas Holcomb was born in Newcastle, Delaware, but his parents moved to Washington, D.C., when he was fourteen and he attended Western High School. Commissioned a second lieutenant in 1900, he spent much of his time as a young officer on the rifle range. For several years he was selected to be a member of the Marine Corps Rifle Team that competed in the annual matches at Camp Perry, Ohio. In 1916 he married Beatrice Clover, a Washington debutante in 1914 and daughter of Rear Admiral Richardson Clover. When war was declared in 1917, Major Holcomb was inspector of target practice at Headquarters Marine Corps but was soon ordered to Quantico to command the 2nd Battalion, 6th Regiment.

Major Holcomb's battalion was the last of the six infantry battalions of the 4th Brigade to sail for France. It had been scheduled to leave in

November 1917 before the 3d Battalion, 6th, but Mrs. Holcomb was expecting her first child. There was a naval saying applicable to Major Holcomb's situation to the effect that, while it was necessary for him to have been present at the laying down of the keel, his presence, although desirable, was not required at the launching of the ship. In this instance, however, headquarters seems to have been sympathetic. The 3d Battalion instead of the 2nd sailed for France in November 1917. All went well. Mrs. Holcomb was delivered of a baby boy. The 2nd Battalion sailed for France in the U.S.S. *Henderson* early in the new year to join the brigade in time for intensive training preparatory to its first stint in the trenches in a quiet sector.

The holidays passed. I was present again at the band serenade on New Year's Day at 1100 at the Commandant's House. I had not expected to be there that year. Something new seemed to occur each day. I learned that I would be within the zone for consideration for promotion to captain by the Junior Selection Board which was to meet early in the new year. That ten days arrest on my record would have been worrisome were I not in my present assignment. (I never found out who recommended me to General Holcomb.)

In the 1930s Washington still possessed much of the quiet charm of a small city. Street cars provided public transportation. For days at a time in summer the heat was severe. The cooling effect of the electric fans which few rooms were without seemed negligible. One bathed upon rising, putting on a clean summer suit to go to duty, only to return sweaty and rumpled in the late afternoon to strip and bathe again. Three or four days each summer the heat and humidity combined to make it impossible for government workers to function efficiently, their perspiration staining the papers on their desks. On such days the federal departments would shut down at noon and all government clerks would leave for the day.

One seldom crossed Lafayette Square without being asked for money, and the donor of a dime was not sneered at by the recipient. The cost of living was correspondingly low. A shirt cost less than $2, a good pair of shoes $8, a Palm Beach summer suit less than $16. A substantial if undistinguished meal cost about 70 cents at Scholl's Cafeteria on Connecticut Avenue where I sometimes had supper toward the end of the month. One could dine well at the Army and Navy Club for a $1.50. I sometimes cashed a check there for $10 which would serve as several days pocket money, but often even $5 would suffice.

Few good restaurants existed except in the hotels. Washington society—cave dweller, diplomatic and State department, naval and military—dined and entertained at home or in their clubs. There was more dancing in Washington then. Many private residences and the embassies had ballrooms. Parents gave dances for debutante daughters. Barnee and his orchestra played nightly at the Shoreham Hotel terrace during the warm months. Thursdays and Saturdays were dance nights at the Chevy Chase Club and the Army and Navy Country Club.

On the last day of March 1937, Colonel Holland M. Smith reported at headquarters to become director of operations and training. Not large but sturdily built rather like General Holcomb, he wore a clipped mustache and eye glasses. Young officers invariably liked him because he was considerate and polite to them, but he was known for his impatience and forceful argument. Born in Alabama, he had graduated from Auburn University in 1901, then studied law for two years before seeking a military career. He was appointed a second lieutenant in 1905. In June 1917, he sailed for France as a captain commanding the machine-gun company of the 5th Regiment. Curiously, although he had been an early advocate of the idea that the naval service should have an assault landing capability and was to do much to develop it, he never served on the staff of the Marine Corps Schools.

In 1936 a board had been convened to make a second revision of the *Tentative Landing Operations Manual*. Colonel Smith arrived in time to review the revised manual for the commandant before it was forwarded to the chief of naval operations and issued as *Landing Operations Doctrine, U.S. Navy, 1937*. During the revision, Captain Chester W. Nimitz, U.S.N., assistant chief of the Bureau of Navigation, conferred frequently with Colonel Smith and appeared several times in the aides' office to keep appointments with General Holcomb. In 1938, still another board of revision was convened. Its report led to the final approved edition which superceded all others. A milestone was passed that year when the Navy published it as *Fleet Training Publication (FTP) 167*. At last there was an official doctrine for landing operations.

In July 1937, seven months after General Holcomb took office, the other key officer he wanted at headquarters arrived. In May, Major General Little, who had stayed on as assistant after General Russell retired, left to command the Fleet Marine Force in San Diego. No general officer replaced him. It had been the custom for the commandant to appoint as his assistant an officer whom he wanted to replace him when his term of office ended. That progression, however, had gone awry when the President selected Brigadier General Holcomb to succeed General Russell.

The new commandant decided that headquarters must function, at least for a year or two, without a general officer assistant. Lieutenant Colonel Alexander Archer Vandegrift, already selected for promotion to colonel, was then finishing his tour as commanding officer of the Embassy

Colonel Alexander A. Vandegrift in 1936.

Guard in Peking. Never suspecting that Vandegrift would one day be his successor, General Holcomb ordered him to Washington to be secretary to the commandant, a new billet created in the circumstance of no assistant.

In June, the senior aide was transferred and replaced by First Lieutenant Cornelius Peter Van Ness with whom I had served in Shanghai. Peter had been General Holcomb's aide in Quantico while a student in the Junior Course. His attractive wife Virginia was well versed in the ways of generals and their wives, as her father, a retired major general, had been quartermaster general of the Army. A few days after being promoted to captain, a much more prestigious advancement then than it is now, I left for two weeks leave in Wisconsin. I returned to find Colonel Vandegrift sitting at a desk in what had been the commandant's office. General Holcomb had moved to the adjacent office, formerly that of General Little.

Earlier in 1937 I had become a White House aide. The winter season of official dinners and receptions had passed when the commandant wrote to the naval aide to the President to propose my appointment. A few days later I was summoned to the office of Captain Paul H. Bastedo, U.S.N., naval aide to the President.

Upon entering the office, which was in the Navy building, I found him in uniform, an unusual sight in the Navy Department. He wore aiguillettes on his right shoulder. My interview with him was largely a formality. He merely wished to look me over and acquaint me with his views about what an officer's attitude should be toward duty at the White House.

One represented one's service at the highest social level of the government. The distinguished, the influential, and the powerful who were invited to the White House would take away impressions, however slight, from their brief contacts with the aides which would enhance or diminish their conception of the naval service. After indicating that I would be appointed, he glanced at his wristwatch and remarked that he was due at the White House in fifteen minutes. We rose together and shook hands as I took my leave. I had reached the door to the corridor when he called out to me.

"Oh, Williams." I halted and turned.

"Sir?" He gestured that I need not retrace my steps.

"I nearly forgot a word of advice I like to pass on to each new White House aide." I waited. He smiled. "Don't bask in the light of reflected glory."

XI

WHITE HOUSE AIDE

Nowadays the press refers to any of the numerous people who have an office in the west wing of the White House or in one of the executive office buildings as a White House aide, but this term used to have a more restricted meaning. It referred specifically to a number of young officers who, while on duty in Washington or posts near the city such as Fort Myer and Fort Belvoir, were assigned additional duty of a social nature at the White House.

A marine officer was first appointed to the position of White House aide toward the end of the last century during the McKinley administration. Unlikely as it may seem, he appears to have been the first naval White House aide. When President McKinley took office in 1897 he appointed Colonel Theodore A. Bingham, Corps of Engineers, to be district commissioner of Public Buildings and Grounds. As such he seems also to have been the President's military advisor and aide. In 1898 Colonel Bingham secured the appointment of an Army officer and one whom he regarded as a naval officer, Captain Charles L. McCawley, USMC, to be his assistants as aides to the President.

Colonel Bingham's decision to ignore all the young naval officers on duty in Washington and select a marine officer to represent the U.S. Navy at the White House had an apoplectic effect in Washington naval circles, departmental and social. Calm was restored when President McKinley, at the suggestion of the Secretary of the Navy, appointed a proper naval officer with stripes on his sleeves instead of on his trousers to be a third junior aide.

For decades White House receptions had been ordeals for senior officials and their wives, the diplomatic corps, and prominent Washingtonians who were expected to attend. No refreshments were served. Ever since President Andrew Jackson had opened the doors to the general public in 1829, the receptions had been mob scenes. Gate-crashers were not turned away. Congressmen brought their boarding house friends and any constituents who happened to be in town. The elite had to rub elbows in the crush with some rather ill-dressed, plain people.

Colonel Bingham, familiar with the pomp and exclusiveness of the courts at Berlin and Rome where he had been military attaché, was determined to change this situation. Although he succeeded in persuading the President to reduce the number of invited guests to 1,000, he was unable to convince him to refuse admittance to those without cards. There was little improvement until after President McKinley's death in 1901, when Theodore Roosevelt took office. During the Roosevelt years, invitations were again received with pleasurable anticipation. The first President Roosevelt appointed a naval aide to the President and increased the number of junior aides. The presidential aides had no other duties outside of the White House, but for the junior or White House aides time spent at the executive mansion was in addition to another full-time assignment. Through the years the number of White House aides was further increased. By 1937 there were twenty. Two of the ten Army aides were Air Corps pilots; two of the ten naval aides were marine officers. Except for the senior aide of each service, a major and a lieutenant commander, all were of the rank of captain (Navy lieutenant) or below. When reporting for duty, we had the privilege of using the north entrance facing Pennsylvania Avenue which otherwise was usually limited to members of the household and the cabinet. We had special licence plates. The numbers from 1000 to 1100 were reserved for the White House. Ours were usually from 1020 to 1040.

Only bachelor officers were appointed White House aides. Sometimes one married at the end of his tour of duty in Washington. The wedding present from his fellow aides was always the same, a handsome engraved silver bowl. When his tour of duty ended and he was transferred elsewhere, an aide received photographs, appropriately inscribed and signed, from both the President and Mrs. Roosevelt.

In 1937, the White House entertainment season of five dinners and five receptions began with the cabinet dinner on Tuesday 14 December, and the diplomatic reception two days later, in an atmosphere of crisis. On Monday the thirteenth the newspapers had reported the sinking of the U.S. gunboat *Panay* by the Japanese in the Yangtze river near Nanking.

President Roosevelt sent a note of protest to Tokyo and the Japanese ambassador called on the secretary of state to apologize for the "mistake."

The diplomatic reception on 16 December was a colorful gathering with many ambassadors and ministers in uniform instead of civilian evening dress. The most striking figure was the dean of the diplomatic corps, the British ambassador, Sir Ronald Lindsay, who stood six feet four. The President and Mrs. Roosevelt, attended by the presidential aides, received in the blue room, standing under the chandelier and facing the south wall. With their backs to the south wall, four aides (known as the four horsemen) faced the receiving line so that the guests passed between them and the President. The arrival and departure of the Chinese and Japanese ambassadors and their staffs were coordinated so that they did not meet. The Japanese were an isolated little group who left soon after being rather grimly received by President Roosevelt. After the last guests had passed through the receiving line there was dancing in the east room to the music of an orchestra from the U.S. Navy Band.

Not all entertainment at the White House was official. Frequently the President and Mrs. Roosevelt invited friends to dine with them in the small dining room. When another man was needed, one of the White House aides would be invited. These were black-tie occasions. There would be cocktails on the second floor with Mrs. Roosevelt. When the guests descended to enter the small dining room, the President would already be seated. One walked up to him and said "good evening, Mr. President," as he shook one's hand.

On 30 December 1937 occurred what was perhaps the best party of the holiday season on the East Coast. The President and Mrs. Roosevelt gave a "small dance" in honor of their youngest son, John, still at Harvard, and his fiancee, Anne Lindsay Clarke of Boston. Four hundred young people were invited, 300 of them men, so the stag line was ample. The aides were invited guests, not on duty, so we wore civilian evening dress.

The President, leaning on the arm of his son Franklin, and Mrs. Roosevelt received together with Miss Clarke and Mrs. Franklin D. Roosevelt, Jr. Eddie Duchin and his orchestra played in the east room. Many small tables were placed in the green, blue, and red rooms where beer and a wine punch were served. To everyone's surprise, the President did not go upstairs until 0100. He sat in a chair near the doorway and seemed to enjoy watching the dancing. The Big Apple was popular then. Toward midnight the young Roosevelts organized a hilarious figure. Some forty men and girls formed a circle from which individuals stepped to "truck." This was a wiggly, shoulder-shaking improvisation with many variations which provoked cheers when well done. The merriest moments

A marine White House aide wearing special full dress uniform in 1938. Officers on duty at the White House wore their aiguillettes on the right shoulder, whereas aides to general and flag officers wore them on the left shoulder. All marine officers were required to have this uniform until the First World War. After that war, this requirement was abolished except for the White House aides who wore the uniform only on the most formal daytime occasions. Courtesy U.S. Marine Corps.

for all, however, were the sight of John Roosevelt doing the shag with his mother. She laughed and protested, but he would not let her go as they hopped about and around at a fast pace to the delight of all.

A new ambassador or minister was received with great formality. It was a brief but dressy ceremony, one of the rare occasions when a marine aide wore special full dress, a uniform discarded by the Corps soon after the First World War except for the two White House aides. A double-breasted frock coat cut short of the knee with sleeves, high collar, and waist belt heavy with gold lace, it had magnificent detachable gold epaulettes and was worn with the gold-striped evening dress trousers.

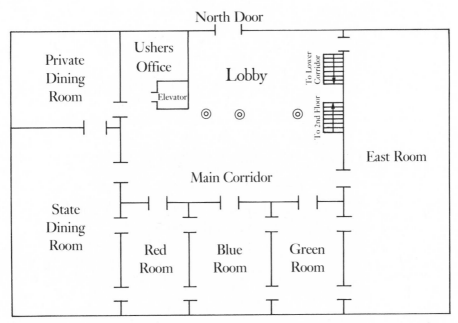

Diagram of the first floor of the White House.

Add gold dress aiguillettes and the special full dress was the ultimate in military finery this side of the Atlantic. These uniform frock coats, dating from before 1917, were passed on from aide to aide. A newly appointed aide would take his second-hand (perhaps actually fifth-hand) coat to a tailor for a fitting and alterations, and sometimes to replace the gold lace, which was expensive.

When he was to receive an ambassador, President Roosevelt left his office to change into cutaway and striped trousers. The senior Army or the senior Navy White House aide accompanied the chief of protocol, George T. Summerlin, to the embassy to escort the ambassador to the White House. As the appointed hour approached, the two presidential aides waited at the elevator while four White House aides waited in the lobby.

The ambassador and his staff arrived at the north entrance. Leaving their coats and hats, all followed the four aides who flanked (two walking slightly ahead to lead) the chief of protocol and the ambassador to the green room. Upon stepping from the elevator, the President proceeded to the blue room where he stood with his two aides under the chandelier facing the corridor entrance.

The four aides then led the ambassador and the chief of protocol, walking abreast and followed by the former's staff in column of twos,

The Honorable George T. Summerlin, chief of protocol 1937–1946. A graduate of the U.S. Military Academy in 1896, he was commissioned a second lieutenant of cavalry but left the Army in 1903 after attaining his captaincy, eventually to make a career in the Foreign Service. In 1937 he was minister to Panama, expecting to retire after becoming sixty-five in November, when a new post, chief of protocol, was created in the Department of State. He was the choice of Secretary of State Cordell Hull, Under Secretary Sumner Welles, and President Roosevelt, who exempted him from compulsory retirement to appoint him. "Summie" to his friends, he was only five feet six inches tall but ramrod straight. Invariably he walked as though marching on parade, and he rolled his own cigarettes.

from the green room into the corridor, turning left and left again to enter the blue room and continue toward the President. As they approached him, the aides fanned out a little, halted, and faced inward so that the ambassador and the chief of protocol passed between them to stop in front of the President. In contrast to the measured pace of the aides (the four horsemen) who escorted the presidential procession at receptions, we marched them at the standard quick step, 120 to the minute.

It was always interesting to hear Mr. Summerlin, a West Point graduate, present the ambassador. There was little time to make his formal introduction as he could not begin speaking until he and the

11 November 1937. Armistice Day ceremony at Arlington National Cemetery. President Roosevelt leans on the arm of Colonel E. M. Watson, his military aide, saluting left-handed. Captain Daniel Callaghan, his naval aide, is a step behind the President. Courtesy U.S. Naval Historical Center.

ambassador were in the blue room doorway, and he wished to finish just as they stopped before the President. Speaking rapidly, he would rattle off, for example, "Mr. President, I have the honor to present (hup, two, three, four) the ambassador extraordinary and minister plenipotentiary (hup, two, three, four) of the Union of Socialist Soviet Republics (halt, one, two).

The President introduced his aides, accepted the credentials, and handed the ambassador his letter acknowledging having received them. The ambassador asked permission to present the members of his staff. When this was done the ceremony was over. The senior White House aide introduced the four aides to the members of the ambassador's suite, while the two principals talked informally for two or three minutes before the ambassador took his leave.

The Army and the Navy approached White House duty differently. Having initiated this duty, the Army seemed to have preserved a superior position, even though the two services were equally represented, by extending the normal two-year tours of duty of the military aide to the President and the senior Army White House aide. In 1937, Colonel Edwin M. "Pa" Watson, a genial field artilleryman, had been the President's aide for some time and would continue as such during the war years

President Franklin D. Roosevelt waves from the U.S.S. *Houston* (CA-30) in 1938–39. Officers to his right are (l-r): Captain Ross McIntire, USN (MC), President's physician, Colonel E. M. Watson, USA, military aide to the President, and Captain Daniel A. Callaghan, USN, naval aide to the President. Courtesy of Capt. Jonathan A. Barker, USN (Ret), 1978.

as brigadier and major general. In some measure, however, this was owing to his being a close friend of the President.

Major Horace B. Smith, Infantry, the senior Army White House aide, was also a fixture. About forty, slight and unsmiling, with a prominent nose, and red mustache and hair, he habitually wore an expression of weary disdain but did a good job of bossing the aides. None of his naval counterparts had his familiarity with Washington faces and form. The Red Fox, as we called him, had spent years in Washington not because he could not be spared from whatever his regular duty was at the War Department but because of his adroit performance at the White House.

My tour of duty of more than two years, however, was unusual for the naval service. During this time I served under three naval aides to the President. The last, Captain Daniel J. Callaghan, a striking figure in uniform with his ruddy complexion and shock of white hair, had little enthusiasm for the assignment but was splendid at it. He was to lose his life during a furious night action off Guadalcanal when a Japanese shell hit the flag bridge of the U.S.S. *San Francisco*. I also served under three senior naval White House aides, for the last of whom, Lieutenant Commander Charles B. McVay III, misfortune waited. Toward the end of the Second World War, he was to lose his ship, the U.S.S. *Indianapolis*, while serving as her captain. At sea unescorted, the ship sank quickly, with great loss of life, after being hit by a Japanese torpedo in circumstances for which he was in some measure held responsible.

One morning in May 1938, as I walked down 18th Street on my way to the Navy Building, it occurred to me that I had been doing so daily for the past year and a half. A year hence, God willing, I should be doing the same but by that time I should be due for permanent change of station orders. My tour of duty at Headquarters Marine Corps was to be extended seven months to achieve a normal June replacement pattern for the aides to the commandant.

It was a pleasant existence, being an aide at the highest military and governmental levels but I was neither gaining experience with troops nor learning more about command and tactics and how to perform the various staff functions. Most of my contemporaries had already attended the Junior Course at Quantico. I had neither participated in a landing exercise nor been educated beyond the Basic School whose curriculum in 1929 contained little about landing operations. My next duty must be school or the FMF. General Holcomb would probably ask me where I wanted to go. I could not ask a former commandant of the Marine Corps Schools to send me to the Infantry School at Fort Benning. The Army school was no longer so desirable anyway, since the FMF had become the most sought-after stateside duty. The Junior Course at Quantico alone offered instruction in landing operations for company grade officers.

In June 1938 Paul Drake left. My old friend of Norfolk Navy Yard and Floating Battalion days, Captain Robert E. "Bunker" Hill, replaced him. A year later, I made my last appearance at the White House on duty, a few days before I was detached from headquarters and ordered to Quantico to be a student in the Junior Course.

Heads of state come to Washington frequently in this age of jet travel, but the state visit of King George VI and Queen Elizabeth in June 1939 was epochal. The royal train from Canada where the King and Queen had made an extended visit arrived at Union Station at 1100 Thursday 8 June. Secretary of State Cordell Hull and the British ambassador, Sir Ronald Lindsay, escorted the royal couple from their railway car across the concourse to the state reception room in the station. There they were received by President and Mrs. Roosevelt with the cabinet and the heads of the services in attendance. The King wore the dress uniform of an Admiral of the Fleet.

The presidential and royal party moved outside to the plaza where honors were rendered by the ceremonial battalion from the Marine Barracks, a battery of the 16th Field Artillery and the Marine Band. Sabres

Start of the state visit of their Britannic majesties, Thursday, 8 June 1939, at Union Station. The picture appears to have been taken a moment after honors were rendered. (The marines in the background are still at present arms). The President, attended by Brigadier General Edwin M. "Pa" Watson, his military aide, draws the attention of King George VI to some detail in the panorama of guard of honor, Marine band, cavalry escort, and field artillery before them. Mrs. Roosevelt and Queen Elizabeth stand to the left and a little to the rear. The two naval officers in the staff rank are from the left, Dr. Ross McIntyre, the President's physician, and Captain Daniel J. Callaghan, naval aide to the President. Courtesy National Archives.

flashed in the bright sunlight as the parade to the White House began. A squadron of the 3d Cavalry from Fort Myer wheeled into column of platoons to lead the escort to Pennsylvania Avenue. The sidewalks were massed and faces appeared in all the windows along the entire route.

I saw none of this. The presidential aides had been at Union Station, but the rest of us were at the White House where the chiefs of mission of the diplomatic corps began to arrive soon after 1100. The world was smaller then. Colonial empires still flourished. There were fewer than fifty countries with which the United States exchanged diplomatic representatives, and only nineteen of these were ambassadors.

We assembled the diplomats in a circle in order of precedence in the east room. The King and Queen and their hosts entered the White House unseen by us via the diplomatic entrance and were lifted to the second floor by the elevator. The aides now lined the corridor. Four of us posted ourselves near the elevator where the chief of protocol waited. Presently the King and Sir Ronald Lindsay appeared. After an interval, the elevator returned with the Queen and Lady Lindsay. Leading the way to the east room, the four aides fanned out to either side of the doorway to halt and face inward as the towering figure of the dean of the diplomatic corps and his sovereign passed and entered the room.

Simple formality prevailed. The ambassadors and ministers were accompanied only by their wives. At state dinners, because of the President's disability, the circle of guests would revolve past him to be received. Now, in his absence, the diplomatic circle stood fast. It took only fifteen minutes for Sir Ronald Lindsay to present his colleagues as he and the King "made the circle," followed by the chief of protocol. Then came the Queen with Lady Lindsay who performed a similar office. No one was late for lunch.

We reported back to the White House at 1900 that evening. State dinners were usually more fun for the aides than other official social events at the White House. There were usually about 80 guests and 150 more invited for the musicale in the east room afterward. During the dinner hour we had no duties and spent most of the time in a room off the lower corridor where coffee and sandwiches awaited us. Before dinner, half the aides were assigned to the east room and half to the lobby. Offering his right arm to the lady of an arriving couple, a lobby aide would escort her and her husband to the doorway of the east room where he would give their names to the announcing aide.

In those days before television, state dinners and receptions had little media exposure. No photographers were permitted to be present. Press coverage was limited to two or three society editors who observed but did not mingle with the guests. Unlike today, no public address system amplified the voice of the aide who announced guests' names to the east room at large as they entered it to be met by a sector aide.

Arriving guests were formed in a circle in descending order of precedence, clockwise with the ranking guests not far from the doorway. The circle was divided into four sectors, each assigned an Army and a naval aide.

Promptly at eight, with the lobby aides lining the corridor, the two presidential aides escorted the President and Mrs. Roosevelt, together with their guests of honor if there were any, from the elevator to the east room. Host and hostess stood just inside the doorway to receive their guests whom Colonel (later Brigadier General) Watson, prompted by a sector aide, announced as they passed between him and the President. After a counterclockwise revolution, the circle broke up as gentlemen sought their dinner partners and Watson led the procession to the state dining room at the other end of the corridor.

On this occasion, I was in charge of the first sector in the east room. Idle for a moment as guests were arriving, I heard the announcing aide intone, "the Commandant of the Marine Corps and Mrs. Holcomb" and glanced toward the doorway to see that Bunker Hill had escorted them from the lobby. It was always an occasion for flashing friendly smiles, even at some distance, when General or Mrs. Holcomb caught the eye of one of his aides in the White House.

When all guests were in place, the presidential aides posted themselves at the elevator. Soon the President, the King, the Queen, and the first lady were standing in line ready to receive. They were a magnificent sight in evening dress. The Queen was breathtaking, quite fulfilling everyone's expectations. Moving to the President's left front, Brigadier General Watson faced toward him. The second circle in the east room that day began to revolve as I moved close behind him to read softly aloud from my sector list the names for him to announce.

After dinner the men remained at table as usual until it was time for the musicale when the President and the King led them back along the corridor to rejoin the ladies in the green room. As the dinner guests went into the east room where chairs for 250 had been placed, Mrs. Roosevelt and the Queen joined the President and the King and the presidential aides in the corridor. They were lining up to receive the after-dinner guests, who were waiting on the stairs and in the lower corridor, when President Roosevelt obeyed a sudden impulse. So far, all had gone smoothly and according to plan. Now, however, something unscheduled was to occur. The President decided that the aides should be presented. The Red Fox forthwith sent for those in the east room and elsewhere to report to the lobby. We fell quickly into line.

The President and those with him moved toward the lobby, away from the entrance to the east room. Major Smith acted as impromptu prompter. Within perhaps two minutes of the moment the President had made his decision, we were clasping his hand, then the King's, the Queen's, and the first lady's. Like everything else in the New Deal, entertainment in the Roosevelt White House was characterized by confidence and flexibility.

A few days later I stood detached from headquarters and proceeded to Marine Barracks, Quantico, Virginia. My bachelor days were also coming to an end. It was arranged for me to report immediately before going on six weeks leave. I returned to Washington and on June twenty-first, my thirty-second birthday, Alice Tuckerman and I were married. Bunker Hill was best man and Captain Samuel B. Griffith II was one of the ushers.

What has been called the interwar period ended less than three months later when the German Army invaded Poland on 1 September 1939, and Britain and France stood by their commitments.

In that same month, Holland M. Smith, promoted to brigadier general, left Headquarters to command the 1st Marine Brigade at Quantico. In 1940 the incredible happened—the fall of France and the evacuation of a British army at Dunkirk. Despite a strong isolationist element, the United States in the last months of that year began a transition from a peacetime to a wartime posture. With the prospect of having to fight in Europe and having no instructional material of its own that dealt with amphibious operations, the U.S. Army reprinted FTP-167, Landing Operations Doctrine, U.S. Navy, *as another of its training manuals.*

On 1 February 1941, the two brigades of the FMF became divisions. Holland Smith became a major general. By the time the Japanese attacked the U.S. Fleet at Pearl Harbor on 7 December 1941, the old Corps was spread rather thin. After that disaster, it disappeared into the rapidly expanding wartime Corps. The peacetime few successfully transmitted their professional skills and habits of discipline to the wartime many, whose peak strength reached 37,000 officers and 447,000 enlisted personnel.

When the 1st Marine Division landed in assault on the island of Guadalcanal in August 1942, Major General Alexander A. Vandegrift was in command. In January 1944, when General Holcomb, having reached the statutory age, retired to become U.S. Minister to the Union of South Africa, General Vandegrift became the first four-star commandant of the Marine Corps. Lieutenant General Holland M. Smith, whom the press invariably referred to as "Howlin' Mad" Smith, initially as commander of the V Amphibious Corps and then of the Fleet Marine Force Pacific, probably had more responsibility than any other officer for the planning, command, and execution of the assault landings across the Central Pacific to Japan. Brigadier General Lemuel C. Shepherd, Jr., led the 1st Provisional Brigade in the assault landing to recapture Guam in 1944. The following year, the brigade having been expanded into the 6th Marine Division, he commanded it as a major general during the Okinawa campaign.

Paradoxically, no marine division participated in the greatest amphibious assault in history. In 1918 a marine infantry brigade under Army command had fought superbly in France against the Germans. Twenty-six years to the day after marines had attacked Belleau Wood, American and British forces landed on the coast of France, the only United States marines participating being members of ships' detachments or observers. It was said that President Roosevelt thought that a marine division should be included in the Normandy landing but that Fleet Admiral Ernest J. King convinced him that all marine divisions were needed to fight Japan. Nevertheless, during the years of peace, the Old Corps had written the doctrine, developed the techniques, and acquired a capability of assaulting a defended beach—prerequisites for the successful Army-Navy amphibious operations in the European Theater that enabled the Army to project its power onto the continent.

EPILOGUE

General Lemuel C. Shepherd, Jr., became the twentieth commandant of the Marine Corps on 1 January 1952. In the spring of 1954 he
ordered me back from Japan to become commanding officer of Marine
Barracks, Washington, D.C. When I first passed through the main gate
two or three days before the change of command to be briefed by Colonel
J.P. Berkeley, whom I was to relieve, the old Barracks looked just the
same as it had in 1935, but I soon learned that there were many changes.

The complement of the post was larger. There were more officers,
especially young bachelor officers. The Marine Corps Institute was located in the Navy Yard. Post activities had a weekly rhythm that culmi-
nated in Sunset Parade on Friday afternoon. There were changes in the
occupancy of officers' row. The only married officer of the post assigned
quarters was the commanding officer. General officers on duty at headquarters occupied the other quarters except number five next to the main
gate. It had been remodeled to provide quarters for bachelor officers and
an officers' mess. Despite its location at one end of the row, it was named
Center House after the old officers' quarters and mess structure that had
stood opposite the flagpole for a century.

Soon after becoming commandant, General Shepherd had initiated
steps to reestablish an officers' mess at the Barracks. Handsome sets of
silver and china, previously ordered, were received about the time I
became commanding officer. All the resources for formal dining were at
hand, so in the summer of 1954 I inaugurated a continuing series of mess
nights, five or six a year, at which all officers of the post were present.
General Shepherd was the guest of honor at the first one.

Mess nights have a double purpose. First, to enable the officers of a
post or unit to dine formally together, making every effort to assure that

A mess night in June 1956 at the Center House Mess. From left to right: Leonard F. Chapman (who succeeded the author as commanding officer of the Barracks), the author, and Colonel "Tiny" Fraser.

each of the elements that combine to make up the whole—food, wine, silver, china, uniform, and service—is of the best. In a way it is like being on parade. Second, to enjoy the occasion and relax with fun and games afterward. Formality prevails until after the toasts.

While observing my first parade as commanding officer with General Shepherd as reviewing officer, I recalled the post parades he had started as a major twenty years earlier. No exception was made then to allow the post flag to fly after sunset so that it could be lowered during the parade. This was possible only during two or three weeks in spring and again in autumn, special occasions which we called sunset parades. Now the flag was lowered during the ceremony every Friday. They were all sunset parades.

General Shepherd had succeeded in institutionalizing the ceremony so that it transcended the dimensions of a mere post parade to reflect the Marine Corps as a whole at its best. There was a drum and bugle corps that executed the British slow march as it countermarched with the band when the two trooped the line after Sound Off. Except on parade days the drum and bugle corps was frequently away from the post for public appearances.

There was also a silent drill team. One platoon of the Barracks Detachment specialized in intricate marchings without command during which its members, with studied nonchalance, tossed their bayonetted rifles around dangerously in complicated variations of the manual. This platoon was also much in demand for public appearances.

All personnel of the ceremonial battalion were about an even 5 feet 10 inches in height. Each year well before the parade season, the barracks detachment commander was ordered to Camp Lejeune and other posts with the commandant's authority to select replacements for marines due for transfer or discharge. There were other refinements. The low-cut issue shoe had a thin sole. It was suitable for wear in garrison and on liberty but fragile in appearance, so the Barracks cobbler had been authorized to double-sole a pair for each officer and man to wear on parade. The uniform for parade was blue, dress, instead of undress. This meant that medals and decorations were worn instead of the ribbons denoting them. They were highly polished. Officers wore Sam Browne belts.

The U.S. Marine Band was under the leadership of Lieutenant Colonel William F. Santleman, a member of the band under Captain Taylor Branson in 1935. His father, Captain William H. Santleman, had been leader for many years before Branson. Some band may at some time have had a drum major equal to Master Sergeant Edmund M. Demar. It is unlikely, however, that anyone who saw De Mar lead the band down Pennsylvania Avenue or at Pass in Review in the Sunset Parade could imagine his peer.

When he enlisted as a trumpeter in 1935, he was warned to stoop when his height was measured. There was a limit of six feet two inches then, and he stood six feet four. He was lean of build with a flat stomach, good chest and shoulders, long legs and arms. His measured step together with the graceful movement of the mace—the whole bearing of the man wearing the silver baldric over the scarlet tunic—always excited admiration and comment. The mace and baldric, which General Shepherd had had made in England, were displayed in the new Center House when not in use. After parade, when he had dismissed the band, Drum Major De Mar would mount the steps to the Center House to return them. Frequently I managed to be there to invite him to have a drink.

The commandant was invariably present in uniform, occasionally as reviewing officer but more often as host to some distinguished person whom he had invited to act as such. He was always willing to consider suggestions, and of course I soon developed some ideas of my own about the conduct of the parade. In good time I proposed certain innovations which he agreed to try.

The execution of fix bayonets by the numbers is a beautiful sight, but it is even more impressive when the drums do the counting. Successive preparatory rolls by the tenor drums precede thumps by the bass drum which replace the oral count. To give noncommissioned officers more prominence, we introduced the dismissing of officers following Pass in Review, after the battalion had reformed and the colors were retired. Company officers returned swords and turned the companies and platoons over to the first sergeants and platoon sergeants. The officers then assembled to march up the center walk and off the parade ground.

We also restored the old Sound Off, again fallen into disuse and forgotten. The band had been playing the usual one of three chords in quick time, but I remembered a more impressive Sound Off by the drums of twenty years earlier. It consisted of three sustained rolls by the tenor drums followed by a double beat of the bass drum before the first downbeat of the music. Each roll began softly, rose to crescendo, then faded with diminuendo. Drum Major De Mar recalled it and soon had the drummers doing it perfectly again.

Finally, we brought back the old "squads right" drill which had been discarded about 1938. General Shepherd's enthusiasm for reviving it faltered when he noticed several imperfections of execution the first time we used it for the parade. Afterwards, we discussed them. I recall that the conversation seemed to be headed toward an adverse decision. I expected it to terminate with something like, "well, it was a good try, but let's return to the regulation drill." Instead, he ended by saying, "well, try it once more, and I'll decide whether or not to keep it." Neither of us detected a fault the following Friday, so the old drill was continued.

About 3,000 people are now admitted to the Barracks to sit in stands to watch Evening Parade. When it was Sunset Parade 600 chairs were set out. The ceremony occurred during the rush hour, and there was no freeway to southeast Washington then. Few people from the northwest section of the city attended except as invited guests. Once, however, despite special preparations to admit as many spectators as possible, the gates had to be closed thirty minutes before parade time.

Sol Hurok, the impresario, brought the regimental band and pipers of the Scots Guards to America in 1955. It was the first of a continuing series of annual tours by different British regimental bands. It was arranged for the musicians and pipers to stay at the Barracks to rest and practice for a few days after flying the Atlantic. (This was before the age of jet travel.) We quartered them in the band hall, the only space available.

Since the Scots were to be with us over a Friday, General Shepherd invited them to participate in the parade. He also invited the British Ambassador, Sir Roger Makins, to review it, and the board of the

Passing in review. Sunset Parade with the old drill. Note the platoons in line of two ranks and in column of three eight-man squads of two ranks.

Sunset Parade 1955 with both the Scots Guards band and the U.S. Marine band participating. The colors are being marched on.

Washington branch of the English Speaking Union to be his and Mrs. Shepherd's guests at the parade and afterward in the garden. It was quite a show, with the Scots Guards Band playing "God save the Queen" at one end of the parade ground, followed by the U.S. Marine Band playing the "Star-Spangled Banner" at the other. After the parade, the pipers took the field in their kilts to delight the crowd with their marching and strange music.

Sunset Parade became Evening Parade in 1957, after I retired and the regulation drill was resumed. Darkness and artificial light add drama and nuance to the parade and enable it to end with a mournful taps as the lights fade. The present day performance sparkles. There are light-hearted moments of joyful noise and incredible dexterity when the drum and bugle corps and the silent drill platoon perform. There is superb marching when the battalion passes in review.

There are other moments of great beauty. The first come when the colors are marched on. A stillness that clings to historic places, usually when only a few persons are present, descends on the crowded stands. The spectators rise as the band, after four beats of the bass drum, plays the "National Emblem," that wistful march seldom heard at any other time. The color guard marches front and center with the national ensign and the battle color of the Corps with its many streamers. The battalion is brought to present arms and the colors are posted in the center of the formation.

Then there are those serene, transcendent moments for the troops at present arms, and for the standing spectators, as the band plays the national anthem with a majesty that other bands never quite seem to equal, as the huge flag descends slowly to be gathered in and folded. There is a mystique to Evening Parade at the old Barracks. It is the ultimate ceremonial expression of the pursuit of excellence in all things military, great and small, of the United States Marine Corps.